Fatherson

Fatherson

A Self Psychology of the Archetypal Masculine

Alfred Collins

Chiron Publications ◆ Wilmette, Illinois

Excerpts from Fyodor Dostoevsky, *The Brothers Karamazov,* translated by Richard Pevear and Larissa Volokhonsky (San Francisco: North Point Press, 1990) are reprinted by permission of Farrar, Straus and Giroux, Inc.

Library of Congress Catalog Card Number: 93–26635

Printed in the United States of America.
Cover design by Michael Barron.
Book design by Siobhan Drummond.

Library of Congress Cataloging-in-Publication Data:

Collins, Alfred, 1943–
        Fatherson : a self psychology of the archetypal
    masculine / Alfred Collins.
                    p.   cm.
        Includes bibliographical references and index.
        ISBN 0–933029–75–6 (pbk.) :$14.95 (est.)
        1. Masculinity (Psychology) 2. Archetype
    (Psychology) 3. Fathers and sons. 4. Men--Psychology.
    5. Jung, C. G. (Carl Gustav), 1875–1961. 6. Kohut, Heinz.
    I. Title.
    BF175.5.M37C65 1993
    155.3'32--dc20   93–26635
                                                              CIP

ISBN 0–933029–75–6

To my father and son
Alfred Collins II (1917–1959)
and
Nicholas Collins (b. 1985)

May you know one another.

Contents

Introduction 1

Chapter 1   The Archetypes' Contested Self. 11
      Senex, Puer, and Archetypal Psychology
      Zen and the University of Chicago
      James Hillman's I and the Fatherson Struggle

Chapter 2   Fatherson Mutuality:
      Kohut and the Selfobject 25
      The Selfobject, the Anima, and Active Imagination
      Eugene Gendlin's "Focusing" and Internal Selves

Chapter 3   Psychoanalytic Fathers and Their Sons 37

Chapter 4   Cross-Bodying:
      Anima and Fatherson as Complementary
      Archetypes of Consciousness 49
      Beauty's Father
      Fatherson and Anima in King Lear

Chapter 5   The Failed Father:
      Old Reprobates and Their Sons 63
      Huck's Pap: Identifying with the Reprobate
      Four Brothers in Quest of a Father:
        The Karamazov Sons

Chapter 6   Fatherson and the King 87
      Iron John's Quest
      Osiris / Horus the King
      The Indian King
      The Father's Death
      Conclusions

Chapter 7   De/Centering and Cultural Cannibalism 113
      The King's Demon in Texas: Robert Caro's
        Lyndon Johnson
      Indian Demons
      Buddhist and Hindu Views of
        the King and Fatherson

Chapter 8   Initiating the Father Through Death 125
              The Father and Son Motif in the Baldr Myth
              Fatherson Initiation in the Katha Upanishad
              Initiating the Demon / Father in
                  the Ramayana *and* Mahabharata

Chapter 9   Toward an Archetypal Self Psychology 135
              The Self Squared and the Order of Selfobjects

             Bibliography 145
             Index 155

Acknowledgments

Thanks to my teachers and readers for enlightenment and criticism. In particular, I wish to acknowledge the encouragement of Terry Gibson, John Beebe, Prakash Desai, Murray Stein, Elaine Molchanov, and Keith Wiger in the development of this manuscript, and the long support of Edgar Polomé and McKim Marriot in my efforts to combine my interests in psychology and Indian studies.

Introduction

*So, from the Father, comes the Son, as the
Father's thought of his own being.*
                                C. G. Jung, Aion, *p. 193*

*[Father to son:] "You are my self with the name
'son.'"*
                        Paraskara Grhya Sutra *1.16.18*
                        (India, ca. 600 B.C.E.*)*

*The self is a relation that relates itself to its
own self.*
                        Kierkegaard, Fear and Trembling/
                        Sickness unto Death, *p. 146*

*A person is not absolutely an individual. His
thoughts are what he is "saying to himself,"
that is, saying to that other self that is just
coming into life in the flow of time.*
                        C. S. Peirce, Collected
                        Papers, *vol. 5, p. 421*

A man's "other self . . . just coming into life," the self in which he
thinks to find or complete *his* self, is often sought in the image and
through the life of his son. Within this patrilineal vision, fathers
and sons are not ideally separate and distinct individuals, as some
recent feminist views of masculine psychology imply (e.g., Chodorow
1978; Gilligan 1982). A son is an other self to his father, who addresses himself (and seeks a reply) in his relation to his boy. The
converse is also true: the son hears himself speaking in his father's
voice and wants to talk back to himself in him. Our lives as fathers
and sons are given direction and meaning by these conversations,
as father and son orient themselves with respect to one another not
only in moments of harmony but also at times of absence, conflict,
and rejection. The fantasy of symbiosis, which is conventionally limited to the mother–infant domain, is not foreign to this masculine
territory, and struggles for—and against—individuation are just as
central here.

In the modern postindustrial West, discord and neglect seem increasingly to dominate the father–son relationship, to the point that for many men the father–son bond has been disrupted, or was never adequately formed in the first place. As the status and role of the Father has been diminished, sons have run wild and free in his absence.[1] This fact has been both celebrated and decried in modern culture. In the 1955 film, *Rebel Without a Cause,* the father is portrayed (by Jim Backus) as a weak and ridiculous man unable to help his troubled teenage son. The son (James Dean) is a sensitive juvenile delinquent who needs a father's strength but gets only pap from his pitifully confused excuse for a dad. The film parodies the family TV shows of the era: it could be subtitled "Father Knows Least." Father and son talk past one another for most of the movie, and it takes the death of a fatherless boy, "fathered" by Dean in the serious play of adolescence, finally to evoke an inkling of strength in his own father and so bring the two—momentarily—together.

If films like *Rebel Without a Cause* bewail and seek to overcome the father-son split, examples of the opposite attitude are also easy to find. Freudian thought has often been interpreted as an attack on repressive patriarchal culture (e.g., by Herbert Marcuse and Norman O. Brown, although not by American medical psychoanalysis, which is a thoroughly patriarchal institution).[2] Groups as diverse as the beatniks, hippies, liberals, feminists, and Marxists share a more or less gleeful contempt for the pretensions of our "hegemonic" cultural Father, and wish to cut him down (a feminist friend once told me about a women's group called SCUM, the "Society for Cutting Up Men"). Recently, the startling—but already fading—triumph of the "deconstructive" school has made this disdain almost gospel in some academic precincts.[3]

---

1. It has been noted that Jungians love to capitalize words. While this can become a bad habit, the upper case does provide a quick and easy means of distinguishing the level of everyday or empirical experience from that of essences or natures. Accordingly, I will capitalize "Father" when speaking of a father principle or "archetype."

2. See Malcolm (1981) and Masson (1990) for amusing discussions of the contemporary psychoanalytic scene.

3. See Lehman (1991) for a well-written, passionate but curiously empty put-down of "deconstruction" and several of its chief exponents.

The anti-Father drive has gone farthest on the ideological plane in the attempt to remove the core canon of Western liberal studies from the center of the university curriculum because it is the work of "dead white men" and perpetuates political control by this class (or its living heirs). The effects on the lives of human fathers and sons are clear. Cosby notwithstanding, the thrust of American popular television has for years been towards denigrating fathers and enjoying cheap laughs at their expense: Archie Bunker and Homer Simpson are typical examples. Philip Wylie (1955) presented an early, sensational recognition of the antimasculine wind's force and direction. The weakened father is not limited to the mass media; he can be found in therapists' offices or, more often, licking his wounds in bars and in the audiences of athletic events. Weak fathers often compensate with brutality, but whether they are outwardly weak or brutal, sons suffer.

The *I Ching* (hexagram 37) remarks that, among the various family ties, the relationship of father and son is most purely a bond of love. The point may be that father and son respond to one another from out of their deepest yearnings for identity or selfhood and love their self in the other person. There follows intense idealization and striving for recognition between them. Because these hopes are often disappointed, father-son rifts and schisms have been prime material for myths and tales around the world. Our current father-son struggles continue the theme, perhaps *in extremis*. In both traditional and modern cultures, the father's essential fantasy is that he can fulfill himself through his son, become through the life of his boy what *he* always intended but could not make actual.

In the end—from the perspective of his death—the father asks his son to make him immortal.

> A father pays his debts to the gods through his son and gains immortality through him. A man enters his wife as semen and in the tenth month is reborn from her as the son. Thus in the son the father's self (*atman*) is reborn from the self, and like a well-provisioned boat he carries the father to the far shore of death. This is the "far-going, auspicious road" where those who have sons walk free from sorrow. (*Aitareya Brahmana* 7.13)

These teachings from an ancient Vedic Indian text are ultimately affirmed in the story of the boy Sunahsepa.[4] In this ancient tale, the father god Varuna demands the sacrifice of an only son by his human father, implicitly as a condition for allowing the father himself to live. Like Abraham, the father acquiesces in his son's slaying (after persuading the god to delay it until adolescence); the boy, however, refuses to let himself be used as the father's ticket from death and runs away into the forest, where he wanders for seven years in pursuit of his own aims. By forging a spiritual tie to the gods during this time, the son in the end saves his father as well as himself and thereby restores the intimate father–son bond. But even when, as here, father–son love finally prevails, fathers' fantasies and those of their sons struggle against each other along the way.

The opposition, or contradiction, of the motives of father and son always turns on the question: *Whose* is this self which we are? To which of us does it belong? In worrying this issue the self becomes a split self, a self versus self.[5] In India, the father–son self conundrum appears in the guru–disciple relationship (gurus and disciples almost always being older and younger males, and often actual fathers and sons). Throughout the Upanishads, and in almost all later Indian traditions including Buddhism, the deepest truth of the self (for Buddhism, the "non-self") is realized by the disciple (*sisya*) only through an intimate, devoted relationship with his teacher (*guru*). Often the guru's words to the disciple reveal the latter's deep self to him, paradigmatically in the upanishadic sentence "*tat tvam asi*" ("You are that [self]!"). Yet the possibility of strife between guru and disciple is implicit throughout the Indian texts and is overt in the much-discussed topic of *guruhatya* (guru murder), one the four most heinous crimes. How can the guru and disciple be held together?

---

4. I have discussed this story at length elsewhere (Collins 1991a).

5. In Shakespeare's *King Lear,* the either-or, zero-sum nature of the "split" father-son relationship is well expressed by Edmund, Gloucester's bastard son, as he betrays his father. He says, "This . . . must draw me [i.e., gain me] that which my father loses—no less than all. The younger rises when the old doth fall" (*King Lear* 3.3). See also chapter 4.

In *"tat tvam asi,"* the son-disciple may hear the father-guru saying, "Boy, you're just a chip off the old block; really not even a chip: there's just the wood block here, and that's me." In Sanskrit, this interpretation would be equivalent to *aham eva tvam asi,* "You are only I." The father-guru would be using the son to affirm his own sense of selfhood and denying the son's independent existence. This would amount to "soul murder" of the son-disciple. And murder is explicit in many Indian stories about evil gurus, of which one is the title story in Heinrich Zimmer's *The King and the Corpse* (1971). An evil mendicant (*sannyasin*) tricks a king into becoming his helper in a black magic rite which aims to imprison all the spirits of the other world and bind them to the mendicant's will. In this ritual, the king is to be the unwitting sacrificial victim. Because of his bravery and presence of mind, however, the king turns the tables on the *sannyasin,* who himself becomes the victim when the king beheads him.

Versions of this story are found in almost every modern Indic language, and in some of these it is clear that the relationship between the *sannyasin* and his helper-victim is that of father and son. In a Bengali version, it is not the king but the "best of his sons" who is given to the *sannyasin.* Furthermore, it is because he was childless and in order to gain a son that the king falls prey to the *sannyasin* (Beck et al. 1987, pp. 79-81). The *sannyasin* represents the dark side of the king's desire for a son, his wish to use the son to prolong himself indefinitely and to enhance his own powers.

But there is another way to interpret *tat tvam asi,* implied in the "non-dual" Vedantic philosophy of Sankara. Here, the phrase expresses an unveiling of both *tat* and *tvam*—a seeing through both guru and disciple to the essence of selfhood within each. In this way, the father's desire for a son, and the guru's for a disciple, imply a kind of suicide rather than murder: in seeking himself through the son, the father-guru sacrifices himself rather than the son.[6] Saying "I" through the son he says "you" to him, a you tasting of an I-ness belonging to neither of them and to both. In other places, the Upanishads express the same matter when the primordial (father) self—the sole reality at the precosmic moment—expresses himself *hantaham,* "Behold: I!" In *hantaham,* the uttered "I" is used by the uttering I as sons are used by their fathers who address themselves

---

6. The great scholar of the "perennial philosophy," Ananda Coomaraswamy, returned continually to this theme of "self sacrifice" (1977, pp. 107-147).

in them, and yet in uttering "I" the I sacrifices himself into it. How is this held together? Who is addressed by the utterance "I"? Am I "I"? As the Zen teacher Dogen said, "To seek the self is to lose the self." In saying "I" there is both a rupture of the I and a necessary fulfillment of it; in being torn apart, the I is held together; it is found through being lost.

My grandfather was lost in the great flu epidemic of 1917- 1918; his only child, my father, was still an infant. Forty-one years later, he too died; I was sixteen years old, my brothers thirteen and seven. I saw Daddy die, his body convulsed by a massive heart attack as I stood in his hospital room, stupidly embarrassed and unable to act. Now, having a son and a daughter of my own, I can sometimes see myself fathering with Dad's mortality and strength, faith and nagging doubt. At times, too, I feel the influence of my little-known grandfather and of an indefinite patrilineage of Texans, Irish, and other men who are utterly unknown to me except that they are my great grandfathers to some exponential degree and partook like me of the strong, black, percolated essence of fatherhood which memory, family tradition, legend, and myth have boiled from the bones of our dads' dads' dads.

Although he did not know his father and had no adequate substitute, my father somehow knew himself as Father. At age four, walking on the campus of Oklahoma City University in the evening with my father, reaching up to hold his hand, I recognized implicitly that he knew me as his son, and so, implicitly, I did also. How sweet it was to be his son at those moments; equally sweet are moments now when I know I am father to my own son. Male humans come to themselves as sons, but we feel our sonship emanating from a father, we see it in the eyes of that man who already has us in mind, already presupposes us because fatherhood runs in his veins.

Father and son as ideas—and their inner correlativity, which I will call Fatherson—are spirits distilled from a generational mash of actual fathers and sons whose personal lives, in the end, were rendered into a whiskey still tasting of their days and seasons. But particular boys and their fathers—this side of the still—are mostly ignorant of the Fatherson essence and drink instead the small beer of personal life lived literally. Enter shame, disappointment, and anger. My own shame in my father arose when he fell from a tower (being attacked by bees) and smashed his leg. For over a year, he was an invalid and after that a cripple. Dad's feelings were hurt when his ten-year-old son would not willingly scratch his leg inside its cast or clean the rank and pussy wound. Each of us imposed literalized images on the other and withdrew love when the other would or could not match the image. I needed Dad to be strong and invulnerable to injury, so that I could be brave in my own small life. He needed me to admire him in spite of his weakness, so that he could keep faith in his male vitality and ability to father us. Neither of us could be what the other thought he needed.

As a result of the magical happiness I felt as a boy with my father, and the rupture of that happiness (only in part the result of his injury and death), I have spent much of my life in quest of the Father. Through the ranks of my gurus, analysts, and teachers (those I have known in the flesh and those I have only read), there winds a red thread: all of my "fathers" have attracted me with their search for a spiritual self. But in one way or another, I have been disappointed in them all and have in turn felt myself less than a good son to each. I have gradually come to accept that father-son strife is as archetypal as love: sons have trouble with the demands of the Father and fathers resist the Son. But the son's struggle with the Father archetype in his dad is one way for him to gain access to the realm of the spiritual self which the Father implies; likewise, the father's conflict with the Son is a way in which the father can approach that selfhood which he intuits in the son. We are Father and father, Son and son. The timeless Fatherson tree sprouts new stories every year, and like the squirrel who runs up and down the trunk of Yggdrasil, we must learn to carry messages between the archetypal root and the offshoots above.

Two of my father figures are psychologists Heinz Kohut and Carl Jung, both primarily in print. The careers of Jung and Kohut run parallel in several ways, each moving from the role of favored son within psychoanalysis to apostate. More significantly, they are both key thinkers in a shift of the Western *Zeitgeist* from what James Hillman has called the "heroic ego" striving to master an impersonal and hostile environment towards a vision of a world—inside and out—filled with selfhood (or soul). The thought of both men circles about the self (or Self) rather than the ego, and for both the relationship with the father (or Father) is an arena in which the self is discovered.[7] Kohut's self psychology remains nominally within the group self of psychoanalysis, while Jung's analytical psychology became the despised Other to the business-suited phalanx of Freudian analysts (cf. Masson 1990). It is not surprising that Kohut has been tarred with the same brush:

> Where Freud only offered to help us exchange unbearable neurotic suffering for ordinary human unhappiness, Kohut opens the door to a strange and enchanted land of make-believe. Why do we find it so hauntingly familiar? . . . . Because we have been there before—it is a return . . . to narcissism; the very narcissism that psychoanalysis had taught us to renounce in favor of the more fragile and yet substantial world of everyday life. (Hanly and Masson 1976, p. 60)

In other words, Kohut has fallen into the pit with Jung. The proud Freudian refusal to see wisdom and harmony as ultimately valid, as more than a momentary and illusory respite from a painful, pleasure-obsessed existence, is indeed inconsistent with both Jung and Kohut, each of whom believed that life has a meaning which transcends pleasure. But it is unfair to claim that either of them denied the brute pain of life or its frequent refusal to meet our wishes, which C. S. Peirce called "Secondness."

The American pragmatic philosopher C. S. Peirce's theories have been increasingly influential in the social sciences of late and provide a useful philosophical context for Fatherson conflict. His theory applies to both linguistic sign and experience with its categories of "Firstness," "Secondness," and "Thirdness." Firstness is direct, unmediated experience prior to subject-object differentiation. Secondness is the sheer "alterity" of the other. Thirdness is, roughly,

---

7. It is conventional wisdom that Jung's thought has little place for the father, and that his theory is essentially one of heroic individuation from the mother (Neumann 1954). If it is true that Jung was disappointed in a weak father—as he himself reported—it would still be odd, in the terms of his own theory, if the father archetype had not made some effort in his life to compensate. I suggest that two places where this occurs in his writings are *Aion* and *Answer to Job*. Homans (1979) has made a good case that Jung had an idealizing transference to Freud (characteristic of sons and fathers), and psychoanalysis sees the relationship as oedipal, with the son Jung as would-be murderer of the more powerful father, Freud.

the experience of the relatedness of subject and object. The Father-son needs Secondness in order to precipitate out as Father and Son in opposition to one another. Their original unity in Firstness can be approached again in Thirdness.

Fathers want sons to fulfill the goals that they think into their boys' futures, but it is *themselves* fathers address in these hopes for their sons. The boy's failure to realize the father's hopes forces the father to recognize his son's Secondness. I recall the perverse pride I felt when my father disappointed me by getting hurt; how individual and full of myself I felt in doing by myself things I had formerly helped Dad to do. In denying his hopes, I appropriated my life for myself. On the other hand, I also recall with pain that Dad seemed disappointed in me and seemed not to understand me. Thus we withdrew from one another, and our Fatherson entered a phase of opposition and strife from which it did not emerge before his death.

CHAPTER 1

The Archetypes' Contested Self

... the energy, the force, the will. Are they one's own, or emanations from the other, from the precursor?

H. Bloom, The Anxiety of
Influence, *p. 52*

As fathers and sons, we struggle for ourselves and for our Self. We live simultaneously in a world of conflict and of quest. Discriminating, while seeking to connect, the conflicting and questing aspects of the psyche was a central concern in C. G. Jung's thought. One of Jung's insights was that each of the fundamental structures or "archetypes" around which the human psyche is organized has the nature of a conscious *person* and expresses itself through images having a personal quality. Every archetype is an "I" and archetypal relations can be understood as a dramatic interplay of love and strife among the members of this family of I's (cf. Jung 1931, par. 360-364; Hillman 1983b, pp. 52-53).[1] The psyche contains a Mother, a Daughter and a Divine Child, a Hero and an Enemy (the Shadow), a Wise Old Man and a Clown, as well as a Father and a Son. The personalness of each archetype is what allows us (human persons) access to its image. This also explains how images work their way under our skin, moving us to see things their way or to fight them for our right to our "own" views. Finally, it is the selfhood of the archetypes that helps us find our self through them.

As the archetypes express their personalities in our lives and individual psyches, they coagulate into the limited structures that Jung called "complexes" and struggle with one another for dominance within the psyche. Interpersonally, one person's complex may strive with the complex of another, leading, for instance, to battles

---

1. This would also be true of psychoanalytic "internal objects," which are like archetypes in relating among themselves—and with the "ego"—as relatively autonomous centers of personality (cf. Greenberg and Mitchell 1985). Eric Berne's transactional analysis is a simplified version of an object relations theory: his "child," "parent," and "adult" are inner personalities who struggle with one another to satisfy their needs.

between the father complex in one individual and the son complex in another (who may or may not be actual father and son). But the singular taste of selfhood is in all the complexes and archetypes, a commonality of nature in the heart which makes it possible for the struggle to reach its resolution. Here, we have named one aspect of this commonality, a unity that lies at the center of the *masculine* psyche, the Fatherson.

SENEX, PUER, AND ARCHETYPAL PSYCHOLOGY

Among Jung's followers, archetypal "personalities" have been emphasized, and perhaps best visioned, by James Hillman and his school of "archetypal psychology" (Hillman 1983b; Samuels 1985). The rubric Hillman uses for the father-son territory is *senex* versus *puer,* or "old man" versus "boy." Within an overall program of seeing through or deconstructing the strong Western ego, Hillman's analysis has viewed the senex as an underlying image of stern habit and rational order, of rigid, ossified law and tradition. But Hillman finds that the senex can never attain *complete* order; his structures are being endlessly "perfected through time" (Hillman 1968, p. 320). The senex is teleologically oriented towards an image of ultimate order and fulfillment which he can never quite reach. Ironically, the perfection the senex seeks is reflected in his antagonist and son, the puer, whose nature expresses a direct, unmediated, and ahistorical vision of spiritual consummation. The puer's flashes of insight tend not to be sustained, and he also, like the senex, needs his masculine other.

In this view, a son image is treasured, by necessity, in the deep heart of a cold senex bureaucrat. Conversely, a wise father sits enthroned in the back of a young iconoclast's mind. In each case, the "conscious" personality unconsciously requires—and idealizes—its archetypal other. The other is kept as an unconscious complex because, paradoxically, it threatens the autonomy of the conscious father or son personality even as it promises to complete it. When one side is rejected and repressed, father and son fight like dogs over a bone—the self-sense is too skimpy to feed both of them, or over too small a doghouse—an identity that doesn't have room for the two of them. One is reminded of the *agon* of the Greek playing field, or the Indo-European poetic contest, or the Amerindian potlatch. A shining halo of I-ness is at stake, something akin to fame, glory, limelight, a sense of kingly grandeur or recognition. To whom will go the self, that golden cup of victory whose wine, it seems, can be drunk by only one but must be poured from the veins of the other?

In Jung's theory, complexes normally possessed only a low level of consciousness, or I-ness, but could act on occasion to take over or assimilate the "conscious ego," which is often imaged as the sun. I-ness thus becomes the prize in an intrapsychic struggle. Usurping the ego's light would be a victory leading to grandiosity and inflation of the complex. From this perspective, all complexes thirst to possess the daylight and to say, like the Buddha, "above the earth and under the sky I am the only exalted one." Each is like a dragon who lies in the darkness hoarding his glittering gold and gems, craving the moment when he can burst flaming into the sky, lord of all he surveys. But the ego is also a dragon: a temporary holder of the light and as puffed-up as any victorious complex. Its light would fail without the unconscious complexes whose I- light it presumes to assimilate. A father-identified ego contends with a son complex struggling to overthrow him; each "knows" who is right in this battle, but how are *we* to choose sides?

As Hillman noted, Jung was ambiguous about the inherent consciousness of the archetypes (1985, pp. 90-91). Most of the time, he limited consciousness proper to ego consciousness and allowed the archetypes—viewed here from the ego's perspective—only a sort of misty "psychic" or "anima" (soul) consciousness. From this perspective, only when the archetypes grow more definite and circumscribed as complexes in opposition to the ego do they achieve a renegade consciousness, the intensity of which is comparable to the ego's. On the other hand, Jung also found the anima, or "soul image," to personify the nature of the unconscious *in itself* as a realm of archetypes possessing their own specific sort of light. Through the anima, the mature ego begins to forge the deeper, cooperative relationship with this "objective" unconscious which Jung called individuation. Hillman—who mistrusts individuation—recommends a polar shift of attention "from I to soul," i.e., from ego interests to those of the anima (1985, p. 93). For him, the two are incompatible. Jung, however, had already undermined this opposition with his brilliant image of the ego as "the mirror in which the unconscious becomes aware of its own face" (1955-1956, par. 129). The anima cannot live without the ego and seeks it passionately. Hillman himself says of the anima that "her first inclination is toward love," to which we only need add "of selfhood" (1985, p. 33).

Jung is close to *tat tvam asi* here: the anima loves and seeks the I, and what she sees in the ego's mirror, her own face, is precisely her I-ness. There is no conflict but rather a union or—better— a nonduality. In herself, the anima can be imagined as the personal quality shared by all archetypes, including Father and Son; she embodies the archetypes' tendency to express themselves through persons inside and out. But there is an I at the heart of soul and of each archetype, and archetypal persons seek this I-ness. The difficulty is that they tend to imagine it as a unique and separate essence. Viewing themselves as "individual" entities, the archetypes and complexes—and humans identified with one or another of these complexes—fight over the I, each seeking it solely for itself. This is the conflict model of the psyche, the realm of the heroic ego. An alternative is to seek selfhood through the anima rather than contesting for it with one's other; this way, Father and Son approach their tertium of shared selfness and can begin to realize a Fatherson.

In his usual, unredeemed position, the senex father chronically seeks I-ness as completion of an insufficient self, "perfection through time." Therefore, for Hillman the project of "individuation," with its aim of achieving wholeness, is marked with the sign of the senex and is beyond the pale of archetypal psychology (1983a, p. 161). We have seen that the senex's completion often entails the (ab)use of his son. The senex is often imagined as an educator or guru towards his puer son, through whom he teaches himself and approaches vicarious perfection. But guruhood has a deep shadow, for within the kindly guru or teacher lies the dark side of the complex, the murderous rage of the zealot who feels compelled to offer up to his "truth" the heads of all those who do not assent to it, if he cannot provide their hearts. On the pupil's side, there is ambition to attain authority and an itch to slay the old king in his teacher.

ZEN AND THE UNIVERSITY OF CHICAGO

One of the finest contemporary accounts of a father-teacher and son and their struggles for selfhood against and through one another is Robert Pirsig's autobiographical novel *Zen and the Art of Motorcycle Maintenance* (1974). The book's form corresponds to a dual purpose: it is a Chautauqua, a traveling lecture course, directed to the reader as well as the narrator's friends and son, on the subject of "Quality," and the story of a man's efforts to reestablish a genuine father-son relationship with his eleven-year-old boy through an extended motorcycle trip into the American West and his own past. Father and son bike across the high country of Montana and are thrown into an intense, but mostly silent, struggle for the soul or spirit the father possessed years earlier when he lived in this place. Our access to the struggle is almost entirely through the reflections and philosophical musings of the father, a former college teacher whose life now revolves around motorcycles and the development of an "owner built" theory of life.

The aim of the Chautauqua gradually reveals itself to be the spiritual salvation of the father-narrator himself and his son through Quality: a direct, unanalyzed realization of spiritual value; thus through a *puer* vision. But darkness and evil shadow the narrative and periodically invade through recollected dreams, flashbacks, and in brute encounters with the narrator's own depression and his son's angry, disturbed psyche; evil especially "comes each afternoon when the new day is gone forever and there's nothing ahead but increasing darkness" (p. 298). At these times, disappointment, guilt and anger, even murderous and suicidal fantasies interrupt the Chautauqua and threaten to overwhelm the daylight vision of teaching and realizing Quality.

Pirsig identifies a dominant perspective of subject-object dualism guiding Western consciousness and traces it back to the Greeks, especially Aristotle, who becomes for him the very image of a smug, all-knowing, and self-satisfied senex: analyst and manipulator of a world seen as outside the self. Mostly unacknowledged, the Stagirite's view of things remains our own, and the culture still sits at the feet of "the ghost of Aristotle speaking down through the centuries—the desiccating lifeless voice of dualistic reason" (p. 360). A contemporary incarnation of the Aristotelian senex is the narrator's former teacher at the University of Chicago, the Chairman of the Committee on the Analysis of Ideas and the Study of Methods. Described by his former students as a "holy terror," the Chairman is also "courtly, grand, with imperial magnanimity" (p. 385); as a good devouring father, he is "well known for graduating only carbon copies of himself" (p. 343).

Like a hero entering the dragon's den, the narrator undertakes to beard the Chairman in his own classroom, across "an enormous round wooden table" with a telling crack running through its middle (p. 361). No easy task, for in place of fire the Chairman breathes

encyclopedic sentences that left subject and predicate completely out of shouting distance. Parenthetic elements were
unexplainably inserted inside other parenthetic elements,
equally unexplainably inserted into sentences whose relevance
to the preceding sentences in the reader's mind was dead and
buried and decayed long before the arrival of the period. (p.
339)

Like the dragon on his treasure, the Chairman's bewildering style
evidently strives to protect some precious nugget within:

The Chairman's statements were guarded—guarded by enormous, labyrinthine fortifications that went on and on with such
complexity and massiveness it was almost impossible to dis-
cover what in the world it was inside them he was guarding. (p.
340)

The naive but brilliant young puer (the narrator's former
personality, who he calls Phaedrus after Plato's rhetorician) suc-
ceeds in confounding the hidebound traditionalist and freeing the
"Quality" which the Chairman (and Greek thought) had kept imprisoned. Phaedrus's puer character is seen in his "fanatic intensity," his devotion to "his one crazy lone dream of Quality . . . for
which he had sacrificed everything" (p. 152). But American opti-
mism ends at this point: Phaedrus's victory brings about his own
downfall. Inflated with the glory gained in his triumph over the
humiliated Chairman, his personality swells, explodes, and col-
lapses; Phaedrus abandons his wife and sons and is committed to
an asylum where he undergoes "annihilation ECS" (electro-convul-
sive shock) designed to erase his personality. When no longer re-
strained or complemented by the senex of tradition, "personal
revelation is preferred to objective knowledge" (Hillman 1968, p.
331). Gravity is transcended, and the puer flies off into the sun.
Heinz Kohut discusses similar gravitational metaphors in the
dreams of his patients. When a patient dreams of orbiting a planet,
Kohut understands him to be too distant from a supportive other;
but even more ominous are dreams of flying off into space, completely ungrounded from any support. Such a grandiose position
must lead to disaster, as with Icarus or Phaedrus.
    Discharged after twenty-eight sessions of ECS, the charac-
ter of the narrator has turned from puer to senex and become a
devotee of Reason. Several years later, he rides in quest of his half-

remembered past life but fears the return of Phaedrus who is now, ironically, a dark and threatening presence. He sees that Phaedrus's "egotism"—like the Chairman's—was his downfall, and he is on guard against ego inflation (puer grandiosity) in himself and especially in his son. Nevertheless, Phaedrus's realization of Quality still preoccupies the narrator. Henceforth, he will be the teacher (of his son, others in the narrative, and us), but also the learner, and in the end a senex-puer integration is at least envisioned.

James Hillman discovers the ego's origin, among other places, in a disorder or inner contradiction of the puer-senex archetype. The ego is the conscious part of the psyche, which becomes inflated with a senex illusion of authority and absolute knowledge (Descartes's cogito is paradigmatic). The unconscious is everything else, and is seen by the ego as both material upon which it can operate—grist for the mill of technique and reason—and as a puer threat to ego's presumed omnipotence. The unconscious from this perspective becomes—ironically—an *objective* psyche, since the conscious ego is the *subject* in the opposition. The way out of the split, for Hillman, lies in the *anima mundi,* a "world" (within and without) that wears its soul on its sleeve and does not need the ego to give it meaning.[2] Intrapsychically, the solution to the subject-object dilemma lies in seeing every archetype as possessing its own intrinsic "ego," i.e., its own structure, meaning, and "I-ness." In this way, archetypes are freed from the necessity of struggling with the ego for a share of the light.[3] By recognizing that archetypes and archetypal images possess an intrinsic selfhood, Hillman "saves the appearances" and makes way for qualities if not Quality.

---

2. This is why he is fascinated with J. J. Gibson's theory of perception, which attempts to locate the interpretive dimension of perception in the stimuli themselves, rather than in some inner "ego" structure (Hillman 1986, p. 44).

3. As he states, Hillman does not like the words *ego* and *self;* hence he would not speak, as I paraphrase him, of archetypes having their own "ego" (1983a, p. 18). They do, however, possess their own "intelligibility" and "order" (ibid., p. 36). Archetypal images do not need any faculty outside themselves to shine, for "they are the psyche itself in its imaginative visibility" (ibid., p. 6); they are "autochthonous" and "independent of the subjective imagination which does the perceiving" (ibid., p. 7). In India, all this would be expressed by saying that archetypal im-

"Motorcycle maintenance" is Pirsig's figure for a way of being in the world that can be both rational and intuitive, both senex and puer. While Phaedrus tried to think his way out of the paper bag of subject-object dualism, the narrator abandons this koan and flows with the machine, "grooving" with his bike like a jazz musician with his instrument. As he tells a friend:

> [The true motorcycle craftsman's] motions and the machine are
> in a kind of harmony . . . . The material and his thoughts are
> changing together in a progression of changes until his mind's
> at rest at the same time the material's right. (p. 167)

But with his son, the subject-object *harmonia* is often absent: the father-son strife present in the narrator's conflicts with Aristotle and the Chairman is repeated with Chris, his own boy; but now the narrator is himself the senex in the drama. With his son he is forced to relive the conflict and raise it to another level. As in many similar tales, the son must learn how to save the father rather than kill him; for his part, the father must learn a lesson similar to the one that Freud recognized, in one of his last papers (1939), as the ultimate proof of psychological health: to accept his passivity and allow himself to be taught.

Early in the motorcycle odyssey, Chris suffers from psychosomatic stomachaches, which have been diagnosed by psychiatrists as "beginning symptoms of mental illness" (p. 66). The narrator rejects this "rational" assessment and intuits that the real problem lies in father–son territory. At this point, his psyche throws up a poem by Goethe which images the situation exactly. As he retells it to his friends:

> A man is riding along a beach at night, through the wind. It's a
> father, with his son, whom he holds fast in his arm. He asks his
> son why he looks so pale, and the son replies, "Father, don't
> you see the ghost?" The father tries to reassure the boy it's only
> a bank of fog along the beach that he sees and only the rustling

---

ages, such as those occurring in dreams, are *svaprakasa,* "self-luminous." Hillman's thought implies that there is no *center,* no origin or focus to the light of archetypes or images: each is evenly suffused by its own light. But does this not contradict his claim of intelligibility and order? How can an archetypal image be intelligible without an I to which the image points or relates?

of the leaves in the wind that he hears but the son keeps saying
it is the ghost and the father rides harder and harder through
the night.

The friends ask "How does it end?" and the narrator answers "In
failure . . . death of the child. The ghost wins" (p. 67).

We recognize the ghost as the shadow of Phaedrus calling
Chris and can guess that his reappearance in the father's mind will
either destroy his relationship with his son or give it new life. We
come to see that the force of death is not Phaedrus but the narrator's
unwillingness and inability to accept Phaedrus and therefore to take
his son seriously, to have faith in Chris, even as he is consciously
striving to initiate him to the ways of Quality. To his father, Chris is
like a mountain climber who is out of harmony with his gear and
life, and who the father must diagnose and cure.

> [The "ego climber"] rejects the here, is unhappy with it, wants
> to be farther up the trail but when he gets there will be just as
> unhappy because then it will be "here." What he's looking for,
> what he wants, is all around him, but he doesn't want that
> because it is all around him. Every step's an effort, both physi-
> cally and spiritually, because he imagines his goal to be exter-
> nal and distant.

That seems to be Chris's problem now. (p. 212)

But the problem is really the narrator's. The father rejects
his actual son and tries to educate him to be the son he wants, the
uncomplaining, tuned-in votary of Quality. Of course, Chris will not
or cannot be this image. Unconscious hurt arises in the father, and
"some anger catches me off guard . . . ." The boy picks this up, and "I
see a sudden flicker of fear in [Chris's] eyes" (p. 215). Fatherson
strife increases, and disgust, resentment, shame, and inner defeat
become dominant (p. 219). Chris cries, and his father seeks an out
through a wishful lie: "Chris, you don't have to prove anything to
me. Do you understand that?" (p. 220). In fact, what is taking place
between father and son is a test as loaded with demands for proof of
fealty as any of the academic confrontations between Phaedrus and
the Chairman.

Things are not always so strained between Chris and his
father, and good times take place in spite of the narrator's efforts to
force them. But often Chris's perceived "ego" rouses the narrator to

a fresh act of rejection (p. 226). Yet the boy keeps up his struggle and gets through to his father in a recurrent traumatic dream referring back to Phaedrus's incarceration in the mental hospital. In the dream, he sees Chris standing on the other side of a glass door and realizes that the boy is afraid: "He's trying to relate to me and is afraid he never will" (p. 226). Chris has been kept awake as his father talks in this dream, telling him, "You said at the top of the mountain we'd see everything. You said you'd meet me there." A few days later, father and son race to a summit, and the son arrives first, proclaiming himself "The Winner!" The narrator comments (now affectionately), "Egotist" (p. 240).

The dream recurs, with the glass door now set in an enormous glass sarcophagus in which the Phaedrus/narrator dream ego is sealed. Chris "motions for me to open the glass door of the vault. I see he wants to talk to me. He wants me to tell him, perhaps, what death is like." Although "a dark figure in a shadow" tries to prevent him, the dream ego shouts through the glass, "CHRIS, I'LL SEE YOU." The boy answers, "Where?" "AT THE BOTTOM OF THE OCEAN!!" Although he is alone "in the deserted ruins of a city" at the dream's end and has pages of father–son turmoil to pass through, this promise of a meeting at the bottom of the ocean seems to presage a breakthrough (p. 273). The dream comes yet again, and the dream ego is able to confront the shadow figure, asking, "By what right is that door closed?" The figure cowers, afraid of him, and he seizes it by the throat "as one holds a serpent." He struggles with it, dragging it into the light to see its face. Of course, it is his face, yet not himself: he recognizes Phaedrus. A kind of *sol niger,* the puer Phaedrus has become the "evil figure in the shadows . . . the loathsome one" (p. 331). But at this point, Chris's voice finally penetrates the glass crypt, shouting "Dad! Dad!" Significantly, the waking and dream ego hear these words simultaneously, for the real Chris is shouting them to his sleep-talking father. The boy has reached his father and has caused his father and Phaedrus to reach one another.

It becomes clear that the narrator's task is to recover his puer and so be able to value the puer in his son. He realizes that

> What I am is a heretic who's recanted, and thereby in everyone's eyes saved his soul. Everyone's eyes but one, who knows deep down inside that all he has saved is his skin. (p. 401)

The Phaedrus of his dreams and Chris in outward life know that the narrator's senex adaptation has been an effort to please the senex of tradition; he was finally shocked into becoming a good pupil of the Chairman. Although his Chautauqua has increasingly mouthed Phaedrus's visions, the narrator has at bottom remained the smug professor unconscious of self who he despises in others. Nevertheless, the inner and outer struggle between senex and puer is bearing fruit, and finally compassion for the puer in his son breaks open the senex heart and the narrator consciously allows Phaedrus to speak through him: "Everything is all right now Chris." "I haven't forgotten you." "We'll be together now." He affirms Chris's stubbornly held conviction that he was never really insane. Through his son's love for Phaedrus's puer spirit, the narrator comes to accept it as himself and to "be one person again": *puer et senex* (p. 409; cf. Hillman 1968, p. 341).

In allowing Phaedrus to live in himself, the narrator becomes able to let Chris live for himself. Symbolically, father and son remove their motorcycle helmets, and Chris stands up on the pegs; for the first time the boy can see ahead on his own, rather than staring into his father's back.

The family of I's in Pirsig's book has four central members: the outer senex (the Chairman), the outer puer (Chris), the inner senex (the narrator), and the inner puer (Phaedrus). Fundamentally, all four are motivated by the quest for Quality, which the narrator compares to Plato's search for the soul (p. 386). All believe in and seek the inner value of our world which is also its source of order and reason:

> Value, the leading edge of reality. . . is the predecessor of structure. . . . Our structured reality is preselected on the basis of value, and to understand structured reality requires an understanding of the value source from which it's derived. (p. 284)

Archetypal and human personalities possess, and paradoxically also seek and struggle over the same, single Quality, soul, or self. In this struggle they succeed, at best, in a momentary flash of glory followed by the ashes of system and power politics. Often there seems not enough Quality to go around, so that it must be hoarded and imprisoned in dogmas and received truths, a typical senex position.

A motto from (and the title of a book on) the French student "revolution" of 1968 is *"sous les pavets la plage"* ("under the paving stones, the beach!"). In the mid-1960s, as an undergraduate at the University of Chicago, I already felt the weight of the paving stones of the academic senex. One humanities professor, in a lecture, let fall the phrase, "The meaning of the poem, properly understood." I do not remember what poem it was or what meaning my professor was trying to convey, but the phrase was like a red flag. For days after, I stewed in my rage that the pompous old fart should presume to tell me the poem's meaning. It seemed clear that the "proper" meaning would be his (or the University of Chicago's) meaning, not mine; I could expect to pay a rental fee for it at the bursar's office with my next tuition check. I despised this scarce, precious, carefully guarded commodity, "proper perception." I wanted the poem to be *mine*, a beach on which I could play (as in Tagore's famous poem) and freely explore. This allergic reaction to authority belongs to the puer, who seeks *his own* visions of Quality, a value whose excellence is inseparable from its being his own creation.

JAMES HILLMAN'S I AND THE FATHERSON STRUGGLE

Sons murder their fathers to make the patrimony their own. Jung's disposal of his own father in fantasy is well known: Paul Jung is imaged in *Memories, Dreams, Reflections* (Jung 1961) as a failed old preacher upon whose church God shits (pp. 39-40), so that the parson's son can play dung beetle in the Lord's night soil and build on the ruins of the Church a neo-pagan tower to the Self. Jung's "treatment" of his father's religious inadequacy has been studied in depth (cf. Stein 1985), and it is clear that Jung's mature thought is in many ways a meditation on—and against—his father's faith.

Two generations later, the future "post-Jungian" James Hillman left Atlantic City and made his passage East; after a few years, he returned from India, leaving a Hindu guru (Gopi Krishna) about whom he later wrote his thesis. Hillman reached Zurich, where—at the end of Jung's life—he became a devotee of Jungian psychology and eventually an heir to its throne. He remained for years an orthodox exponent of Jung's thought until he found his own archetypal voice. Such at any rate is the story I extract from his book *Inter Views* (p. 112). Hillman gradually took exception to Jung's emphasis on the relationship between the personal ego and the self and has for years sawed away at this ego-self axis, which many would consider the centerpost of analytical psychology. In rejecting the son role toward Jung, Hillman reached for his own selfhood.

Hillman attacks the father's ego/self ideas, which Jung considered the backbone of his theory, and preserves the theory's disarticulated body parts (the archetypes freed from the structural constraints imposed by the self). The positive result of de-selfing Jung's work is to allow a freer and fuller view of archetypal images in themselves; ironically, however, it also risks losing the center of selfhood in each archetypal phenomenon, and specifically in Hillman's image of himself as a psychological thinker.

It is clear that Hillman deeply reveres Jung, but I believe he has trouble with the "Jung's-ness" of the older man's psychology. He sees Jung in the mythical role of founder but denies that he himself has assumed a founder role in his own "archetypal" psychology. In fact, Hillman's work constantly attacks the myths of the "heroic ego" and "individuation," with its emphasis on what he sees as a static and final wholeness. He does not want to be a wise old man. In *Inter Views*, "Laura Pozzo" asked him about this issue:

> In your book *The Myth of Analysis* you wrote that Freud behaved like the founder of a religion, or a sect. You are a Jungian who has stepped out from Jungian orthodoxy and founded a new school, archetypal psychology. Don't you think you are in the same myth in which Freud was, the myth of the founder? . . . .You are quoted, invited to speak. You have a following and pupils . . . . (Hillman 1985, pp. 27, 28)

Hillman's response seems disingenuous:

> But as to followers, as you call them, the fantasy is more that I feel myself a member of a body, a community . . . a kinship with people who work with similar ideas or at least are trying to revision things . . . .These people are not followers, not "my students." . . .They are friends . . . . there is nothing else to call them. Friends. We are all sort of in love with each other. (Ibid., p. 28)

Hillman later acknowledged his discomfort with the myth of the founding father: "The 'me' is protecting himself against this goddamn James Hillman. I don't know how to carry this founding image gracefully" (ibid., pp. 112-113). Hillman contrasted his sense of his own "smallness" with the gigantic mythical father Jung, who because of his size can carry the image easily (ibid., pp. 103-104). In a men's conference with Robert Bly, Hillman made a significant exception to this sense of smallness: he said that his *head* always felt big and was hard for his skinny neck to carry. A swollen head (inflation, grandiosity?) isn't easy to manage, but cutting it down to size is an extreme solution.

Hillman's aim seems to be to dissolve the Self into the archetypes, and the archetypes (deprived of their individual nuclei of selfhood) into archetypal images. He would thereby avoid the struggle for the self which fathers and sons know all too well. But the Fatherson struggle only moves onto another plane in his writing as Hillman the son tilts against the four-armed windmill of the father's self.

How are we to understand that archetypes such as Father and Son, puer and senex, anima and animus, intrinsically are I's and yet fight like dogs over the I when they are not seeing their I through the I of their other? Jung's psychic complementarity and Jung's and Hillman's notion of the syzygy are helpful, and we will find that Kohut's seminal idea of the self-selfobject relationship gives even greater conceptual clarity. The fantasies of love and strife are not exclusive. The I might be viewed more like a verb than a noun, a verb not exclusively transitive or intransitive. "I-ing" may have to do with the self of the other as much as with myself. At times (as with the self- contained, twilight consciousness of the archetypes in their "natural" state, or in the moment of supreme self-realization) the I may seem intransitive, independent of any other self; at other times (as in the filial struggle of puer with senex) it may seem transitive, establishing itself at the expense of the self of the other, or through the latter's love. Reconciling the transitive claims to selfhood of the various archetypes would then be the main project of myth.

CHAPTER 2

Fatherson Mutuality
Kohut and the Selfobject

I and my father are one. (John 10:30)

This book makes use of two main sets of tools: Jung's archetypal perspective and the self psychology of Heinz Kohut. We used an archetypal tool—the puer-senex relationship—in the previous chapter to look at the Fatherson, particularly through the case of Robert Pirsig's Phaedrus. This chapter concerns a tool from the second box: the self-selfobject nexus as understood by Kohut.

Heinz Kohut's idea of the *selfobject,* while limited by its embeddedness in the tradition of Freudian psychoanalysis, is useful in understanding the mutual or shared selfhood we see in relationships such as that of father and son. The concept of selfobject centers on the insight that an *empathic* tie exists between the selves of persons and the most significant parts of their environments (parents, spouses, children, etc.). Although Kohut developed the self-object idea over a lifetime, and treated it in various ways in different writings, empathy between self and selfobject is always an essential aspect of it. A typical definition is this:

> Selfobjects are objects which we experienced as part of our self; the expected control over them is, therefore, closer to the concept of the control which a grown-up expects to have over his own body and mind than to the concept of the control which he expects to have over others. There are two kinds of selfobjects: those who respond to and confirm the child's innate sense of vigor, greatness and perfection; and those to whom the child can look up and with whom he can merge as an image of calmness, infallibility and omnipotence. The first type is referred to as the mirroring selfobject, and the second as the idealized parental imago. The self, the core of our personality, has various constituents which we acquire in the interplay with those persons in our earliest childhood environment whom we experienced as selfobjects. (Kohut and Wolf 1978)

The cohesiveness of the self (corresponding, in classical Freudian terms, to the strength of the ego) depends on ongoing, life-long relationships between the self and satisfactory "mirroring" and "idealized" selfobjects. Kohut's late writings stress that healthy adults, as much as children, require from their selfobjects an ongoing empathic resonance: "A basic in-tuneness must exist between the self and its selfobjects . . . . The experience of the availability of empathic resonance [is] the major constituent of the sense of security in adult life" (Kohut 1984, pp. 70, 77). The selfobject environment is approached by a healthy self with a sort of Eriksonian "basic trust" in its capacity to mirror and to be idealized. In psychoanalytic patients who lack this trust due to an unempathic childhood environment, successful treatment "leads to the patient's increasing realization that, contrary to his experiences in childhood, the sustaining echo of empathic resonance is indeed available in this world" (Kohut 1984, p. 78).

Kohut for years posited two distinct kinds of selfobject. In the above quotation these are called the "mirroring selfobject" and the "idealized parent imago" (elsewhere termed the "idealized selfobject"). At the end of his life, Kohut added a third type, the "alter ego" selfobject, who is experienced as "someone who is sufficiently like [me] to understand [me] and to be understood by [me]" (1984, p. 196). Kohut does not make this connection, but he may have created the alter ego selfobject from a sense that the relationship to all selfobjects is *mutual* rather than unidirectional. Selfobject relationships make better sense when viewed as implicitly reciprocal. For instance, when a boy admires (idealizes) his father, thereby enhancing the *boy's* self, he simultaneously mirrors the father, enhancing the *father's* self. There is a mutuality between self and selfobject such that the self's mirroring selfobject is simultaneously a self seeking an idealized selfobject in the "original" self.[1]

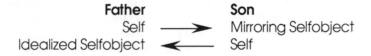

The addition of the alter ego selfobject adds other possibilities of self-selfobject mutuality, the simplest being that self and selfobject each feel themselves to be "twins" of the other. A frequent

1. In psychoanalytic treatment this implies that the analyst who mirrors the patient's self seeks and receives selfobject support by idealizing the patient. Kohut touches on this issue in discussing the "overvaluation of the patient" (1984, p. 190).

empathic intervention during psychoanalysis described by Kohut is to affirm to the patient that the analyst is like the patient, e.g., "we are all sensitive . . ." (1984, p. 176).

The son arrives in the world as his father's selfobject and, through this experience of selfobjecthood, realizes himself as a self. But this strongly implies that there is a mutuality (a syzygy, to use Jung's and Hillman's term) between self and selfobject such that there is inherently a selfhood in the selfobject and a selfobjecthood in the self. A *tertium* between self and selfobject was intuited by Kohut and coagulated literally in his theory as a third type of selfobject. This hypothesis is confirmed by the strong emphasis in his late writings on an "empathic in-tuneness between self and selfobject" (Kohut 1984, p. 66); their mutuality had been less emphasized in earlier versions of Kohut's theory. Even in the later theory, however, a genuinely equal and two-way self-selfobject bond is reserved for a developmentally advanced stage in adulthood, exemplified, for instance, by a successful marriage (ibid., p. 220).

Kohut's thinking also shifted over time from a greater to a lesser emphasis on psychic "structures" and internalization. In *The Restoration of the Self* (1977), for example, Kohut emphasized the "nuclear self," the psychic organization of the self around *ambitions* and *ideals,* goals derived respectively from mirroring and idealized selfobjects, which guide the person's subsequent life and give it meaning. In his final book (1984), the focus is on the quality of mature self-selfobject relationships between persons and their families, cultures, etc. While selfobjects that will actualize the self's ambitions and ideals are still important, it is the fact of a secure, trustworthy "path of empathy" between self and selfobject that interests Kohut most at this point (1984, p. 66); the specific ambitions and ideals which mark the path have become somewhat peripheral.

Kohut's theory suffers, like Freud's, from an excessively extraverted orientation. If it is true, as Stein (1976), Satinover (1987), and others have asserted, that Freud's "narcissism" is homologous to Jung's "introversion," then it is ironic that, for Kohut, "narcissistic" needs can only be met from outside, through environmental selfobjects. Kohut's theory would be stronger if he had considered the possibility of "internal," intrapsychic selfobjects as well as environmental ones (see Collins 1991b; Bacal 1990, p. 216). In fact, an entree for such an addition to his theory is readily at hand in Kohut's early equation of introspection and empathy (defined on occasion as "vicarious introspection") (1978, p. 206).

In one of his first important papers, Kohut claimed that the psychological domain is *defined* by empathy and introspection: "We designate phenomena as mental, psychic, or psychological if our mode of observation includes introspection and empathy *as an essential constituent*" (Kohut 1959, p. 209). Empathy came to be viewed in his mature theory as the essence of the relationship between self and selfobject and seems to lie at the heart of the argument in his last book. Although Kohut does not say it, introspection could also be looked at in this way, with the selfobject being internal in the case of introspection. Approaching this insight, Kohut occasionally speaks of "empathy for oneself" (1971, p. 305; 1984, p. 72); this is introspection as a self-selfobject relationship, not merely a means of gaining knowledge, a window of access to the inner world. The latter would be a "technical" and partial kind of relationship, not one engaging the whole self. Empathy could be understood technically also, and Kohut sometimes seems to use the term in this way (1971, p. 300). But only when analyst and patient are in a genuine self-selfobject relationship can interpretations based on empathy succeed: the self-selfobject relationship is primary; empathic interpretation is a carrier of the relationship within which it occurs (Kohut 1984, p. 176).

Perhaps the reason Kohut ignores the possibility of genuine (psychically "objective") internal selfobjects is that he identifies many internal structures as defensive. Narcissistic personality disorders are in fact defined by the psyche's attempt to achieve a grandiose self-sufficiency and independence from external ("real") selfobjects through a merger in fantasy with internalized selfobject images, typically an all-mirroring parental imago (Kohut 1977, p. 208). The self innately requires selfobject support and, in its absence, attempts to hold onto an imagined "internal" selfobject. If successful, the person acquires a narcissistic personality; if unsuccessful, the person becomes psychotic. Kohut concludes that healthy adults (and cured narcissists) leave internal selfobject structures behind and come realistically to believe in the selfobjecthood of (part of) the environment. The possibility that intrapsychic selfobjects might be *objective* (in Jung's sense, i.e., not the defensive creations of a threatened self or ego) is never considered by Kohut.

Jeffrey Satinover reaches an even more negative position following the same assumption that only external, environmental selfobject support could meet the needs of the self. According to Satinover, the demands of the archetypal Self are so overweening and the world so unempathic to them that an "intolerable conflict" is generated, and the person is driven to defensive solutions such as projecting the Self onto a God image (1987, p. 104). Satinover implicitly rejects the possibility of a "good enough" selfobject environment and limits the category of selfhood to the impossible demands of a childish but archetypal Self.

The quotation from Kohut and Wolf (1978) cited at the beginning of this chapter states that selfobjects are persons in the outer world who are experienced as part of our self, similar to our experience of our body and mind. This equation can be reversed to view the body and mind as (similar to) selfobjects. In fact, once the inner/outer barrier has been lowered in this way, it becomes possible to see the entire psychic and physical world as a realm of selfobjects. A psychology extracted from Indian philosophical texts makes this much more plausible (Collins 1991b, 1991c): from this view, "internal" and "external" phenomena are of the same fundamental nature (*prakrti*), and all exist for the sake of a self (*purusa*) to whom they are selfobjects. The fundamental cleavage (and potential *coniunctio*) in our experience is not between "internal" and "external" but between self and selfobject, the latter including both inner and outer contents. Body, mind, mother, father, even culture: all are selfobjects.

But although the person and his world are selfobjects, not all parts of the environment are selfobjects of the same value. As Kohut realized but only occasionally discusses, some selfobjects are *traumatic* rather than supportive of the self (Kohut 1984, p. 220). Psychoanalytic object relations theories such as Melanie Klein's (Segal 1964) call traumatic selfobjects "bad" and supportive ones "good." Correlative to good and bad selfobjects, the self can be (in Kohut's terms) "cohesive" or "fragmented."

I have tried to recast Kohut's theory with three major changes: self and selfobject are seen as related *mutually* rather than in one-way fashion (as when the selfobject supports the self but not vice versa); selfobjects are *internal* to the psyche as well as part of the interpersonal environment; and selfobjects (and selves) can be "bad" as well as "good." But the fundamental issue for Kohut's thought, as it must be for all psychological thinkers, is one of faith (cf. Grinnell 1970): Is a good enough selfobject—whether psychic or environmental—available to me? Kohut and Jung both have faith that what Winnicott called "provision" (recalling the Christian "providence") is available, but Jung's faith was more in the psyche while Kohut primarily believed in the possibility of empathic resonance from the outer world.

THE SELFOBJECT, THE ANIMA, AND ACTIVE IMAGINATION

Selfobject theory, especially as I have modified it, can be usefully applied to many of Jung's ideas, with much profit to both theories. I will look at two Jungian ideas that offer a potential of overcoming the Fatherson struggle over self-ownership and power: the *coniunctio* and active imagination. A third notion, the anima, is perhaps the most important of Jung's antiauthoritarian concepts and will be discussed in chapter 4.

The alchemical *coniunctio* is expressed in heterosexual imagery in the *Rosarium Philosophorum* (Jung 1946): the King and the Queen are locked in coital union in the atmospheric space above the moon and under the sun (which participate in their joining). Jung and Schwartz-Salant (1987) interpret the King and Queen to represent the "body" and the "mind," or ego and anima, and certainly it is difficult to perceive traces of a Fatherson dynamic here. But after the *coniunctio* comes death, the *nigredo,* and here it is easy to see the effects of a fight-to-the-death struggle like that of the negative Fatherson. In the *nigredo,* self-selfobject mutuality is lost after a prior union, but paradoxically this absence of union looks like an even closer bond. Thus, the *Rosarium* images the *nigredo* as a *fused* King-Queen lying in a sarcophagus. Union between self and selfobject carries the danger (or inevitable consequence) of a "merger" state (Schwartz-Salant) in which self or selfobject is absorbed by the other. In the Indian tale "Sunahsepa," a human father (obeying the father god Varuna) was tempted to resorb the son for whom he had prayed, using him as fuel for the flame of an extended life. There is a necessary and inevitable confusion between the "empathic resonance" or "in-tuneness" between self and selfobject which Kohut considers the highest state of psychological development—and which corresponds closely to the *coniunctio*—and a fusion state in which the self absorbs the selfobject, or is eaten by it.

Why does the *coniunctio precede* the *nigredo?* Many myths and philosophies express this "psychic fact" which Mircea Eliade has called the "fall into history." For India, the earlier stages of creation are higher and better than later ones and less dominated by self-selfobject strife. Late stages of the world are imaged by the "law of the fishes" (*matsyanyaya*), where bigger fish eat the smaller. In the Indian analog to the Greek Golden Age, the Krta Yuga, people spontaneously follow *dharma* (the law of harmonious social mutuality), while in the Lead Age, or Kali Yuga—which we now inhabit— selfish egotism (*ahamkara*) dominates our social interactions. In Kashmiri Saiva thought, the world process is described as a devolution from a conscious self-selfobject (Siva-Sakti) unity, called *vimarsa,* to a "contracted" state where Siva-consciousness is imprisoned in the material world. Microcosmically, the initial stages of *all* psychological processes are more Siva-like while their late stages tend to be "contracted" and unconscious. The insight is that contraction (merger) of self and selfobject is *inevitable,* although with tantric disciplines it can be reversed (and will, in any case, be reversed at the "end of history" when the contracted world is burned in the light of Siva's rekindled consciousness). The *nigredo* is a contracted state but could not exist without the prior occurrence of self-selfobject mutuality, the *tertium* between "the polarities of fusion and distance" (Schwartz-Salant 1987, p. 140) which is the *coniunctio.*

Fatherson harmony, as when Pirsig's narrator consciously accepts both his puer and senex aspects, is ontologically *prior* to Fatherson conflict, although "in history" its attainment is a return. From the perspective of the struggle between father and son for a bigger slice of the pie of selfhood, the Fatherson *coniunctio* is a golden memory, and achieving it is indeed a "work against nature."

Active imagination is not merely a technique of Jungian therapy; it is perhaps the essence of the transformative process as understood by Jung. In active imagination, the patient's ego confronts his archetypal unconscious in a true self-selfobject relationship, one in which the self and the selfobject terms are not permanently identified with ego and archetype. Hillman cites an instance of active imagination where an elderly man was addressed by an inner child with the words, "Where have you been staying, Father?" (1983c, p. 88). The man (as we would all be strongly tempted to do) rationalized the encounter, striving to reestablish ego control over the unconscious image. But what he should have done, according to Hillman, was simply "to hear the child's question—where had he been?—and try to respond to it" (ibid.). The man was not the self in the encounter but the selfobject; the child needed something from him, but he refused to allow himself to be used and lost the possibility of union. In the play between the archetypes and the ego, and among the archetypes, everyone is sometimes self and sometimes selfobject. It might be a definition of the ego to call it a giving in to the temptation to claim the self role *permanently*. Ego would then be the *nigredo* tendency, the principle of contraction, which is to say in Freudian terms that its nature is the death instinct.

A memory both precious and painful from early childhood is a dream I had of a wonderful, magic land and of blue jewels I found there and held in my hand. Waking, I tried to bring the jewels back with me, but as ego consciousness replaced the dream world I realized they weren't really in my hand. Growing disappointed and hurt, I held on tighter and tighter to the jewels, my fist contracting to hold off the truth of its emptiness. I lay there for several minutes not daring to open my hand.

Active imagination rests on trust in the internal selfobject, faith that mutuality with it is possible. Because this requires giving up, or allowing oneself to see through, the pretension of the ego to exclusive selfhood, active imagination is difficult. But to say this is to fall into the very reason why it is "difficult," for active imagination is not something that the ego simply *does,* through free exercise of its sovereign powers. Active imagination is equally something which is *done to* the ego, and this "being done to," when it is against one's will, is psychopathology. Hillman's emphasis on the diseased and weak aspects of the psyche reflects the fact that the ego is constantly engaged in a sort of "passive imagination" with the archetypes, who talk to it, as Jung and Hillman show, through diseases. The refusal to be selfobject to the archetypes is thus destined to failure. The father will not be allowed to use up his son in order to remain himself forever (in "Sunahsepa," the father who attempted this instead fell ill with dropsy). Likewise, life will not permit the son to cling forever to the illusion of "being his own source"; sooner or later, the world's Secondness will grind this daydream away, leaving in its place paranoia or a stress disorder. Illnesses are what the archetypal world is saying to us; when the patient listens willingly, sickness can become active imagination.

The archetypal perspective inhabits the psyche with many centers of selfhood, and so with multiple selfobjects. Self-selfobject interactions ricochet around the psyche in a circle game, and the psyche is "a theater of personified powers always implicating each other" (Hillman 1985, p. 169). There is self in every selfobject (it could not be a selfobject otherwise), and every self is first a selfobject. Long ago I had a dream that rather frightened me: light had somehow entered into a many-sided "mirror box" and was eternally reflecting back and forth among the mirrors inside. I was struck then by the obsessive, repetitive quality of the image, but I admire it now as a neat bouleversement of the ego, for every mirror—like every archetype—is both self and object to every other. Jung compares the deep psyche to a

> world of water, where all life floats in suspension . . . . where I am indivisibly this and that; where I experience the other in myself and the other-than-myself experiences me . . . . There I am the object of every subject, in complete reversal of my ordinary consciousness where I am always the subject that has an object. (Jung 1954, par. 45-46)

EUGENE GENDLIN'S "FOCUSING" AND INTERNAL SELVES

The multiselfhood of the psyche, and the possibility of overcoming the contractions of the ego pretense, are suggested in quite different language in the work of Eugene Gendlin (1985, 1987). Writing from the client-centered tradition of Carl Rogers, Gendlin develops Rogers's idea of "openness to experience" as a way beyond the contracted self concept (or rigid ego) within which we generally operate. The key notion for Gendlin is the "felt sense," which he defines as a "complex kinesthetic sense," "feedback" coming from the "body," which at every moment offers a view of a person's state independent or complementary to that of the ego (1987, pp. 278, 281). Attending to the felt sense and responding to it (often in words) is called "focusing."

Gendlin provides examples from psychotherapy sessions which greatly help in understanding the process. Successful focusing often means that a person lets go of the ego's view and gets in touch with an "unclear body sense" which grows more definite in commenting on past relationships of the ego with others in the person's life. In one example, a woman formulates herself in this way: "So it's like I keep trying out my worth on him and keep coming up against 'Yeah, I like you, but'" (Gendlin 1987, p. 280). The client's ego has been trying to demonstrate its "worth" in the eyes of a pro-

spective mate; now, *for the first time* she realizes this and also sees
that all along she has implicitly felt his rejection of some aspects of
her. As Gendlin notes, the ego imposes an order on experience but is
unconscious of this. An implicit awareness of the ego's projects exists, however, as part of an "intricate order" in the "experiencing" of
the body or psyche (of which the ego is part). In focusing, the person
cooperates with this intricate order, allows it to function through
him and become "focused"; seeing himself (his ego) for the first time,
in the context of the body's sense, the person becomes able to reject
old patterns of control. In our example, the woman becomes free to
let go her old pattern of trying to achieve worth through the esteem
of her man (which she had not been aware she was doing). The felt
sense provides a stance from which the ego can be seen and, in
Hillman's phrase, "seen through." In this way, the ego changes.

In selfobject terms, focusing turns the tables on the ego's
pretense that it is the only self in the psyche; in the focusing process,
the felt sense in fact takes the ego's place as self and the ego becomes (when focusing is successful) a cooperative selfobject. Gendlin
emphasizes that focusing is a process of *"steps,"* and we can see these
as the ongoing, mutually reflective process of the psyche, in which
the self of the moment will be the selfobject of the next moment,
which will develop in turn into a self seeking further selfobjects. The
dialogue between ego and felt sense is essentially identical with active imagination, if we can legitimately identify Jung's archetypal
psyche with Gendlin's "body." At first, this may seem difficult, but
functionally the body and the archetypes play homologous roles in
the two theories: each compensates for the one-sidedness of the ego
and leads the person into a developmental process of many steps
(called "individuation" by Jung). As we saw, psychological "faith"
can be placed in the psyche or in the environment; Gendlin has simply placed his trust in the *body,* which can readily be viewed (like
the "polytheistic" psyche or the human environment) as a selfobject.[2]
We may add, for good measure, that *culture* also plays a corrective
selfobject role (Winnicott 1971).

Returning to the Fatherson, we can see more clearly now
that Father and Son attain consciousness through the mirror-play
with one another. Gendlin's ideas help us to see that this "conscious-

---

2. Recall that Kohut speaks of a "body-mind self" and defines selfobjects
as parts of the environment which we treat as if they were parts of our
minds or bodies (Kohut and Wolf 1978).

ness" is also a *development* for both Father and Son; "steps" of this development can be seen in the masculine life cycle and in the generational succession of actual fathers and sons. Perhaps it is their mutual reflection over time that "expresses" or "distills" an "essence" of Fatherson, to refer to metaphors used earlier. We are in a better position to appreciate the exclamation of a Vedic Indian sage, whose realization of spiritual reality took a Fatherson form in saying, "I was Manu [the first ancestor and primordial Man] and the sun!" (*Brhadaranyaka Upanishad* 1.4.10). In another text of the same period, the sage Mahidasa Aitareya imagines the origin of the world and his connection to it in Fatherson language: "This world was [in the Beginning] water. This was the root, that the shoot. This the father, those the sons. Whatever there is of the son's, that is the father's; whatever of the father's, that is the son's . . . . I know myself as reaching to the gods and the gods as reaching to me" (*Aitareya Aranyaka* 2.1.8). The Fatherson *tertium* or essence is imagined as the sun, or water, or Manu. It was "always" so, but only for those who (now) know (in Sanskrit, *ya evam veda*). Consciousness of what eternally is (Jung's archetypal dimension) arises only for those sons who reflect on their origins, and for the Original Father only through the eyes of his sons.

CHAPTER 3

Psychoanalytic Fathers and Their Sons

The "son" (putra) is the one who "saves" (-tra) a
"man" (pums-) from death.

             Sanskrit folk etymology

The self . . . demands sacrifice by sacrificing
itself to us.

             C. G. Jung

For Freudian psychoanalysis, Oedipus is still king. The son's guilty struggle with his father remains the dominant motive in male human life, and our culture speaks with father's voice. This seems odd, or perhaps anachronistic, in a world where the masculine is expressed in images of macho ferocity (Rambo) and wimpy sensitivity (Alan Alda) but rarely as mature Father. In fact, the decline of Father (and the brutality or weakness of the masculine diminishing him) seems to underlie a recent psychic upwelling in this area. Robert Bly writes:

> The old anger against the father, so characteristic of the nineteenth century and earlier centuries, has been replaced in many men by a kind of passivity and remoteness, which springs from a feeling that the father has abandoned or rejected them. (In Mahdi 1987, p. 190)

Has he died? The theme of the dead father, and of desire for the death of a living father, are central to the Freudian Oedipus complex. Freud discussed two dreams, one concerning the death of a father, the other the death of a son.

> A man who at one time had looked after his father through a long and painful illness up to his death, informed me than in the months following his father's decease he had repeatedly dreamt as follows: *his father was again alive and he was talking to him as of old. But as he did so he felt it exceedingly painful that his father was nevertheless dead, only not aware of the fact.* (Freud 1911, p. 28)

A father had been watching beside his child's sickbed for days
and nights on end. After the child died, he went into the next
room to lie down, but left the door open so that he could see
from his bedroom into the room in which his child's body was
laid out, with tall candles standing round it. An old man had
been engaged to keep watch over it . . . . After a few hours sleep,
the father had a dream that *his child was standing beside his
bed, caught him by the arm, and whispered to him reproach-
fully: "Father, don't you see I'm burning?"* He woke up, noticed
a bright glare of light from the next room, hurried into it and
found that the old watchman had dropped off to sleep and that
the wrappings and one of the arms of his beloved child's body
had been burned. (Freud 1900, p. 509)

The first dream of the "dead father" seems clearly oedipal;
according to Freud, it is to be understood in terms of "the infantile
significance of the death wish against the father" (1911, p. 27). But
the dream is also based on the son's love for his moribund father and
his wish that the father be released from his suffering. In the dream,
the father is dead but does not know it. The son wants the father
both dead and not dead (he sees the father alive because he wishes
to deny his death, as well as his own death wish toward the father).
In the second, "dead son" dream the father's love for his son is the
dominant emotion, but psychoanalytic theory would suggest that
the father's rivalrous and even hateful feelings toward the son would
make this love also ambivalent. Also, it is not clear from Freud's
text that the child is in fact a son, but Lacan, in his discussion of the
passage, assumes it (Lacan 1960).

George Devereux (1953) has called the father's oedipal hatred of the son the "Laius complex," after Oedipus's father. In Greek
myth, Laius was cursed to be killed by his own son (who would
marry his mother, Laius's wife) as punishment for Laius's homosexual rape of the boy Chrysippus, son of King Pelops. Devereux
argues that Oedipus and Chrysippus are homologous figures, and
that Oedipus's murder of his father is in fact retribution for the
father's aggressive homosexual attack on his alter ego. Of course,
Laius acts aggressively toward Oedipus also, by exposing him to the
elements in infancy and by piercing his ankles—for Devereux, a
castration symbol. In good psychoanalytic fashion, Devereux
equates homosexual domination with castration and cites evidence
that Oedipus symbolically "turns the tables on his homosexual father, by castrating . . . and feminizing him" in the act of murdering

him, "as he (Oedipus) had once been castrated and feminized (pierced ankles) by Laius" (1953, p. 134). Oedipus's behavior—and, by implication, oedipal behavior in all boys—is "induced by the behavior of his father" (ibid.). The motive for father's behavior on Devereux's theory is purely instinctual: he is driven by aggressive and homosexual impulses. It would not be hard to read such motives into the father in the "dead son" dream. As Gallop suggests, burning is often a metaphor for sexual passion or violation (1985, p. 180).

A. K. Ramanujan, in part following Goldman (1978), builds a strong case for father-son relations in traditional India being primarily of the Laius complex type: fathers aggress against their sons and demand that the sons "transfer [their] political and sexual potency" to the father (1983, p. 244). In a famous example from the great Indian epic, the *Mahabharata*:

> Bhisma, the first son of Santanu, renounces both kingdom and his reproductive life so that his father may marry a fishergirl and continue his (father's) sexual reproductive life. Bhisma, lifelong celibate, lives on to become the most revered old man of the epic, warrior and wise man. (Ramanujan 1983, p. 244)

The renunciation is demanded by the father, Santanu, and seems to result in Bhisma assuming the role abandoned by his father of being the "old man"; the rejuvenated Santanu becomes, conversely, a functionally *young* man. Similar examples can be found (see Ramanujan 1983 and Goldman 1978). The son's self-sacrifice or submission to the father is a "culturally favored" oedipal resolution in India and is seen among contemporary Indians as well as in myths and fairy tales (Goldman 1978; Carstairs 1967; Roland 1988).

Ramanujan summarizes his argument:

> We see that the Indian and Greek tales . . . do not differ in the basic pattern: (a) like sexes repel, (b) unlike sexes attract, across generations. But they do differ in the *direction* of aggression or desire. Instead of sons desiring mothers and overcoming fathers (e.g., Oedipus) . . . most often [in India] we have fathers (or father-figures) suppressing sons and desiring daughters. (1983, p. 252)

Pulling some of these threads together, we have a two-way Oedipus-*cum*-Laius complex, with the father desiring something of the son's and aggressing against him to get it, just as the son does toward the father. However, it is not clear what this "something" is. There is simultaneously love and hate between father and son, although psychoanalysis can only understand the love in terms of passive/active homosexual desires (Devereux 1953; Goldman 1978). Most striking to me is that fathers live through their sons when they use them sexually (homosexually usurping their virility) and so assimilate their identities, just as sons in classical Freudian thought conversely identify with their fathers (the ego's relation to the ego ideal has a passive homosexual quality). Perhaps the homosexual theme might be better understood symbolically (in Jung's sense) as a metaphor for a sharing of selfhood (rather than semen) between father and son. Moreover, semen is often understood as the essence of the person and hence literally *as the self*. Given this, the struggle to be the homosexual impregnator rather than the one impregnated is easily viewed as a case of Fatherson struggle to be the self half of a self-selfobject relationship rather than the underdog selfobject.

This theme of homosexual impregnation has strong resonances of initiation, where Fatherson struggle is less central than Fatherson transmission across generations. We can see this mythologem today in the moving if slightly ridiculous form of the "men's weekends" led by Robert Bly and others. Bly, who is a fine poet and writer, becomes guru and shaman at these events, where he offers himself as a psychic father to his middle-class audience of generally younger men in quest of male selfhood. Bly's favorite exemplary image is "Iron John," a fairy-tale wild man who carries off an eight-year-old boy and initiates him into the male virtues of self-denial and martial prowess. In the end, Iron John is revealed to be a king and adopts the boy (now a young man) as his heir by promising to give him "all the treasures I possess" (Colum 1972; see also chapter 6). Reports of the Bly weekends note that rough language and farting seem to be ways in which male bonding is achieved. Bly himself is viewed as a lovably crude, foulmouthed Dad who cuts through the citified, sissified cortex and reaches primitive centers of masculinity deep in the psyches of his boys. Bly's appeal is not only to the olfactory sense; he chants and plays the lyre, and dresses in colorful garb.

As a child, age twelve, I used to take daily walks with a somewhat older friend, and we would taunt the "Old Gentleman" (as he named God) to strike us down before the next telephone pole if He was really up there in the sky among the sun dogs, galaxies, comets, and meteors that we young astronomers knew to be the *real* occupants of heaven. Even then I can recall a wistful felt sense that the Old Gentleman might be worth more to me than my cynical inflation.

Lacan's analysis of the dead father and dead son dreams quoted above argues that oedipal anger (the "death wish") covers and defends against a more profound issue: the wish to protect the father from death, because the Fatherson unity implies that the father's death is also the son's. To kill the father, Lacan argues, is to turn passive into active: it is an identification with the aggressor, who is not the father but whatever it is that kills him before I do. This, for Lacan, is the death instinct, understood as a force of unconsciousness. Gallop notes: "As long as the father does not know he is dead, he can be present, but as soon as he knows, he will disappear; as soon as he knows, he is lost" (1985, p. 158).

The death instinct is the force that leads to the knowledge of one's own death, which implies one's own unconsciousness. The ego defends itself and its Father against this fading into unconsciousness, which is our nature, by hiding his death from the Father, and by making itself his killer.[1]

Perhaps we have come here to the world of the *nigredo,* of the ego's contraction. Desiring not to know its death, the ego presumes to know all, to be the single sun in the starry night of the psyche. The secret (unknown to the ego) is that in contracting around its own emptiness it affirms that emptiness and achieves the unconsciousness it thinks it seeks to avoid. We do not know that

---

1. "Fading," a key term in French poststructuralism, is based on a concept of Heidegger's. The idea is that the ego (ego-illusion of "mastery") is in the process of dissolving, or being seen through, in the course of the argument. In the Indian Vedanta system, the personal ego is seen through at the moment of enlightenment; we could say that it fades away as the absolute consciousness shines through it, "sublating" the ego, to use a common term for this process. Poststructuralism, however, has no place for an absolute: fading of ego subjectivity eliminates an illusion or resistance; it does not put another reality in its place.

we are motivated by the death instinct in our most "daylight" moments, when we strive to be our (ego) selves. But for whose sake is the ego's death, and the Father's?[2]

I argued in chapter 2 that the psyche is a family of selves-selfobjects, each seeking its self through and against others. The death—or its psychic equivalent, unconsciousness—of any archetypal selfobject is likely to signify life to some other archetype. The Father's death is, at one level, the (son's) ego's life: this is the Oedipus complex. Conversely, the ego's death gives life to father: the Laius complex. In selfobject terms, to be conscious is to be the self of the moment, and to be unconscious is to be the selfobject (like the moon which only shines by reflection of the ego-sun's light). The death instinct is an instinct of self-sacrifice or surrender to the reality of being "for another's sake" (Sanskrit *anyartha*) and not "for one's own sake" (*svartha*); it is the acceptance of being a selfobject. And always, in the nature of things, this means to support the selfhood of a self appropriate to one's selfobject qualities. Lacan almost recognizes the sacrifice implied in the dead father dream: "Rather than have him [the father] know [that he is dead], 'I' would die" (1977, p. 300). In Gallop's words: "by preserving his father's ignorance, the dreamer wishes to make it a dream of his own death" (1985, p. 171). But for Lacan, this is only a hubristic turning of the father's passivity into the ego's activity—albeit suicidal activity. I prefer to see a genuine sacrifice here, one which aims to preserve Fatherson as a whole by surrendering to Father's I.

To summarize, the constricted, grandiose ego seeks to be the only self and to find selfobjects outside; if this ego is a son, he seeks to make the father his selfobject. The self-sacrificial son-ego reverses things and seeks to be for the sake of the father (who is now treated as the self rather than selfobject). In Kohutian terms, the grandiose ego seeks mirroring, while the sacrificial ego seeks to idealize. Each is one-sided, and to that extent unconscious.

To view the death instinct as a self-sacrificial move aiming to achieve a sort of vicarious selfhood through enhancing the selfhood of an idealized other may seem odd, and it is certainly un-Lacanian (not to mention un-Freudian). However, exactly such a process is at the root of "enlightenment" as understood by the

---

2. In Joseph's words, we are moving from a "psychology of absence" to a "psychology of presence" (1987, p. 10).

Sankhya school of Indian philosophy (and by other Indian schools as well). For Sankhya, the psycho-physical world as a whole is called *prakrti* (primordial Nature) and exists solely "for the sake of" a second basic principle, *purusa* (spirit or the Person) (Larson 1969). *Prakrti* is entirely unconscious but acts so as to evoke consciousness in *purusa* of his true nature, which is, precisely, consciousness. All the workings of the body and mind, as well as of the external world, are solely aimed at this realization. A series of images is given in the primary Sankhya texts to illustrate the *purusa-prakrti* relationship. Perhaps the most telling is the comparison of *prakrti* with a female dancer and *purusa* with her male spectator. *Prakrti* dances to show *purusa* that she does not exist; the purpose of her dance is to fade (in Lacan's sense), to signify the absence of a true subjectivity in herself. As she says to *purusa* in the *Sankhya Karika,* "I am not; there is no 'I' in me; nothing is mine." But there is an I in *purusa,* and thanks to the fading selfhood of *prakrti* he knows it.

Although Sankhya does not say this (and "consciously" denies *purusa's* need for *prakrti*), I believe that *prakrti's* nay-saying of herself exemplifies a new type of selfobject relationship, which I have called the *negative selfobject* (Collins 1991b, 1991c). The term *negative selfobject* was suggested by psychological learning theories in which a "negative" reinforcement (reward) is achieved by the removal of a noxious stimulus. The latter would correspond to the "bad" or traumatic selfobject, the removal of which is experienced as a self-affirmation. The negative selfobject, then, is one which reveals that the badness which it or another selfobject seemed to reflect onto the self does not exist, or has no connection to the self. Like all selfobjects, the negative selfobject lives in a mutuality with its self and participates in the self's selfhood. Just so, the father and son interpenetrate and support one another mutually even as one, motivated by the "death instinct," sacrifices himself for the other.

We noted above that the *nigredo* ego, whose essence is the death instinct, is necessarily unconscious of its nature. In Sankhya, too, *prakrti* is unconscious. How then can she realize her nature *as unconscious?* Lacan's fading of the ego provides an image of the paradox involved in speaking of "consciousness of one's unconsciousness." Although Lacan, as far as I can see, never leaves the level of paradox (which may explain the magician persona of his later years), a resolution of the paradox is possible through the experience of psychic faith.

In the previous chapter we noted that Kohut, Gendlin, Winnicott, and Jung all base their vision of psychological health on the faith that an appropriate selfobject, of one sort or another, will be provided for a person when it is needed. For the fading ego, that selfobject may be expressed as the father (or son), but this will prove insufficient at a later time, since the father fades, too, and in fading implies a brightening son (or other archetype). Ad infinitum. This is the world of my mirror box: selves and selfobjects reflecting one another forever. For Fatherson, it is the world of the generations succeeding each other endlessly. There can be faith of a sort here, the "faith" of harvested grain that next spring its seeds will live again. A deeper and more satisfying faith for the ego, and for *prakrti,* would involve a realization of the light in the box, which does not change its nature as it bounces about. To realize unconsciousness implies that unconsciousness is a selfobject—a *negative* selfobject—to consciousness. It says "I am not" to the I, which is I through this communication. Faith would be placed in the light that sees me when I do not know it and because I do not know it.

Sankhya speaks of this as if it were a once-and-for-all event: *prakrti* dances, and is seen, and then never dances again, for in this moment *purusa* attains realization of his ultimate "solitariness" (*kaivalya*). This sort of instantaneous enlightenment is characteristic of much Hindu and Buddhist thought, but not all, and I have tried to show that it represents an inadequate or one-sided view of the matter (Collins 1991c). As Harvey Alper says:

> The Hindu tradition itself, on the level of theory, distinguishes *moksa* as a goal from those skills or techniques which are employed, intentionally or tacitly, to attain it . . . . this distinction must be called into question. The distinction between path and goal appears to be putative . . . . The only thing that may be observed is a process of continually "deepened" renunciation which has a beginning but not, apparently, an end. (1979, p. 26)

In my view, realization does not have an end because it always depends on a negative selfobject and, therefore (like all self-relevant phenomena), is necessarily a two-sided event. The consciousness that realizes "I (ego) am not" ("I am unconscious") is not the negative selfobject that says this. And yet, it is the saying of this which is the self-sacrifice that allows it to be realized.

Let me provide an illustration. In *Star Trek,* Captain Kirk and crew frequently "beam" themselves up and down between the space ship and the planet they are visiting. I have always wondered why no one seems afraid to enter the transport chamber where bodies are dissolved into pure energy so that other, identical bodies can be fabricated in another place. There is no problem with arriving, assuming that all one's fingers and toes are in order; one simply realizes, "I'm not on the *Enterprise* as 'I' was a moment ago; I'm on Altair Four." But voluntarily allowing one's body to be chopped to atoms in an electronic meat grinder is another thing altogether. The faith required to step into the transporter chamber for the first time would seem immense, assuming any imagination on the part of the transportee. The metaphor is this: the person entering the transporter is like the negative selfobject, saying (as he literally fades) "I am not"—a scary thing to do. The realizing self is like the person who arrives, saying to himself, "I am not (on the *Enterprise*)." Even though the person exiting the transporter is different from the person who entered (they presumably do not share a single atom), they are also the same. Without the self-sacrifice of the person entering the transporter, the ("other") person could not exit, breathing a sign of relief that "I" made it.

For some Indian schools of thought (especially Buddhists such as the Yogacara), all life is literally like our *Star Trek* image: we are burned away at each moment, and our new self of the next moment is merely a causal effect of the earlier one. The point of emphasizing the discontinuity of our "momentary selves" (which carries over to discontinuity between father and son generations) is to drive us to place our faith in a higher level selfhood: *nirvana* or "emptiness" (*sunyata*) for the Buddhists; *purusa* or *atman* for Hindus. But even in this case enlightenment is logically not once and for all: at each moment we are required to step again into the transporter.

This realization "I (ego) am not" is a cause for overwhelming joy if one "believes" in "mind" (as a Zen text puts it). I knew this one night soon after I entered graduate school in Austin, Texas. "In a dream I realized the truth of emptiness": these were the words with which I expressed the experience the next morning. As I recall, I had the thought "everything is empty" and then *realized* this, at which moment I felt myself and my world explode into light and joy. The thought and experience of emptiness recurred perhaps ten or twelve times over the next half hour, and once was accompanied by the visual image of a tangled knot of thread being pulled straight with a snap. As the knot unraveled, I again dissolved into light.

How did I let myself go into that "good night"? No doubt being asleep helped, relaxing the ego's grip. But since age thirteen or so, I have somehow implicitly known about the joy of emptiness. I recall reading Alan Watts's *Spirit of Zen* and shivering in recognition when he spoke of *mu* and *satori*. Shivers of another sort, intimations of ghostly visitation, plagued me a few years later, following my father's death. Although at the time I shrugged it off, I have not forgotten that in the year or two before he died, my father talked to me about his coming death and tried to convey to me his faith in what lay on the other side. He said something like, "I don't know what is after death, but I am curious. I am not afraid of it." I didn't really listen, but now I think my father could have walked into the transporter.

Oedipus/Laius is about the self primarily, and about hatred, homosexual rape, and incest only because these are ways that the Fatherson self expresses itself *in extremis*. To focus only on the extreme expressions would be, in Kohut's terms, to be caught in the "breakdown products" of a self deprived of adequate selfobject support. If the self is intrinsically fading into an "other" self, we could equally say that it is "breaking down," and that its "breakdown products" are part of the (new) self. The difference between a fragmented self in Kohut's sense and a fading self (in modified Lacanian terms) is faith and consciousness. If my focus is on the fragments only, then consciousness contracts to conform to their contours; I do not (allow myself to) see beyond their horizon; I "believe" only in them. Addictions are like this: the alcoholic worships his booze, thinks of it obsessively, but never considers what the craving really seeks. Seeing what one's self-fragments point toward, however, relaxes the constricted idolatry or perversion: the drunk in Alcoholics Anonymous lets the all-too-solid bottle of whiskey fade, along with the ego who holds it in a death grip; he sees them no longer as their "own source" but as potential selfobjects of a higher powered self. The relief of letting go, surrendering the ego, is sweet and transformative, but why does AA insist that an alcoholic is *always* an alcoholic, even if he has not taken a drink in many years? My argument implies that it is because the fading (recovering) alcoholic obsession remains a necessary selfobject to the person's higher power; once recovered, the former alcoholic would become inflated with the arrogance of "being his own cause" and therefore prey to a new addiction.

I have discussed the Oedipus complex with hardly a mention of mother. In fact, Fatherson (as Bly and Hillman note) has apparently no place for her, yet for Freud she motivates father-son hostility. I have claimed that selfhood is the bone of contention between father and son; for Freud it is a woman (in the standard oedipal complex this is the mother; in the inverted Oedipus or Laius complex it can be the son's wife, sister, etc.). Who is correct? Actually I believe that a symbolic reading of Freud, and of the role of women in a culture that puts men in the foreground, dissolves the disagreement.

Lévi-Strauss (1969) propounded the idea that women are a medium of exchange through which (groups of) men are related. In particular, in the "atom of kinship" a man is related, through the sister whom he gives in marriage, to his (now) brother-in- law. Diagrammatically:

The atom of kinship idea partakes of Lévi-Strauss's general principle that cultural forms (especially myths, but also kinship systems) strive to overcome an irresolvable contradiction. In this case, the contradiction is between the claims of the man and of his brother-in-law. Assuming that the urge toward incest is universal, the man naturally desires his own sister. Giving her to another man is a loss to him, and to make the loss bearable the other man is treated to some extent as a second self, a sort of *de jure* brother. In cross-cousin kinship systems, a lineage of males exchanges women with another lineage, so that the loss of a woman in one generation is made up in the next (Lévi-Strauss 1969, pp. 119-145).

But incest itself is more than a sexual matter, and we may see it as an attempt to unite the self in a bond so tight that it dispenses with the need for a selfobject. In the *nigredo* image we have exactly this: the incestuous *coniunctio* of King and Queen results in their fusion into one body. The atom of kinship, then, might be viewed as incest one step removed and made homosexual rather than heterosexual. But the matter could also be understood symbolically, as we did in concluding that Devereux's homosexual father–son tie is really about the selfhood of the father and son. The atom of kinship then would also be about the finding of selfhood through another man, in this case the brother-in-law.[3] Oedipal Fatherson itself could also be defined as an atom of kinship, with mother taking the place of sister as the medium of relatedness (and conflict). The oedipal atom could be diagramed:

This emphasizes the mother–son descent: the father–son tie (the dotted line) comes later and is more a cultural matter than either the marital tie of the parents or the birth relationship of mother and son. But this suggests to me that the feminine principle, far more than a mere medium of exchange, might be seen as another sort of *tertium* between the males—an essence of their selfhood—both in Lévi-Strauss's "atom" and in the Fatherson. And this leads back to the anima.

---

3. In the *Bhagavad Gita*, the reluctant warrior Arjuna is initiated into his true selfhood by his guru and charioteer, Krishna, the avatar of God Vishnu, who in human form is Arjuna's brother-in-law and also cross-cousin (his mother Kunti's brother's son):

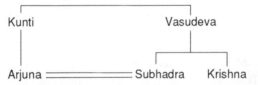

This is the standard South Indian kinship pattern, but in the *Gita* it also represents the tie between a man and his deep masculine self, imaged as a kind of older brother–younger brother rather than father–son relationship.

CHAPTER 4

Cross-Bodying

Anima and Fatherson as Complementary Archetypes of Consciousness

Some years ago I had a powerful dream, the cognitive content of which was that God was female. I recall the rush of ecstasy which accompanied an image of Her as a young woman and simultaneously an imageless but absolute presence, somehow female, that I sensed very near me. I was saved from being rendered entirely into feminine light by the grace of the young woman, who told me that we must remain a few inches apart. The taste of union remained unconsummated (or the union unmerged), and so I lived to tell the tale.

Just a few days ago I had a similar dream. My wife was being initiated by two very beautiful Indian women into a certain spiritual state or *"loka"* (this Sanskrit term for "world" was used in the dream). It was made clear to me that I was allowed, as a privileged outsider, to experience this *loka*. I held back at first but then let go my fears and ego-attachment and seemed to rise into a space of light and bliss that was, as in the earlier dream, feminine. The experience was accompanied by words, in this case a Hindu *mantra*, and was repeated a number of times.

From the perspective of such experiences the male world of Fatherson almost seems a defense against the feminine principle, a desperate attempt to hold onto the masculine ego by tracing its lineage back to the (male) gods. But before throwing in the locker-room towel, let me ask: what do "masculine" and "feminine" signify, anyway? James Hillman, following Jung, raises the excellent question "whether we can truly speak of the anima *per se* as feminine . . . Paradoxically, the very archetype of the feminine may not itself be feminine" (Hillman 1985, p. 65). His point is that anima in itself is prior to femininity, and especially prior to the femininity of men, since anima also occurs in women. For this reason, Hillman compares anima to the Hindu concepts of *maya* and *sakti,* cosmic principles which create the "world" (for the Hindus, always a psychic world, a world inhabited by consciousness). Maya and Sakti are also represented in Hinduism as goddesses, but not just goddesses: each is simultaneously a cosmic power.

Earlier we explored the Fatherson *tertium* in terms of a *coniunctio* between the father and son, a harmony or distilled spirit. But if father and son each finds himself through a woman, or in a feminine essence or power, we may question whether the Fatherson, a central archetype of the masculine, is itself *essentially* masculine. In fact, like the anima's femininity, Fatherson may be a cosmic power that exists prior to maleness. Perhaps, given enough energy, we can even see the two cosmic powers combine.

"God is a circle with center everywhere and circumference nowhere." This mystical aperçu is relevant to the self but is only half right as applied to it: an adequate self theory must have a place for a circumference aspect of selfhood as well as a center aspect, and (the hard part) must connect the two. There is a vastness to anima, like an endlessly expansive horizon, and the self-luminosity *(svapra-kasata)* of the dream state. But the anima is all circumference; she has no center and flows everywhere like a will-o-the-wisp: "This vaporous soul substance, like the mists that hang over marshes . . ." (Hillman 1985, p. 19). She is the archetype of the selfobject, of the *mundus* that radiates selfhood: anima consciousness is characterized by "an attachment to something or someone else to which it is an echo" (Hillman 1985, p. 23). There is a sweet promiscuity about her, for anima gives self to all, but also takes away the single selfness of each. She makes a world that glows from one edgeless edge to the other, and so is an *unus mundus* that is "one" only in the sense that the light suffusing it does not end. In the terms of perceptual psychology, anima might be called a *ganzfeld,* a "total field" or featureless perceptual field.

> The *ganzfeld* image suggests a snowy whiteout and calls back a dream of mine from many years ago:
> In the wilderness in winter, a ruddy man lived alone with his fire in a cave. When the fire went out, he left the cave and stood outside while snow fell. He lay down in the soft snow, face up, and I looked at the whitish sky through his eyes. I saw the swirling snow fall onto my face and eyes as I relaxed in its cold comfort. I felt beauty and ease.

I think this was an anima dream, partly because of the beauty of it and partly because of the self-sacrifice of the ego's focal energy (the fire) and abandonment of self to the aimless flakes of snow. In the dream, a center (the cave with its fire) gives way to periphery and horizon; there is a dissolving of self in the world, a movement from ego to *anima mundi.*

Fatherson as such is not peripheral, and its light does not diffuse into the atmosphere: there is a centeredness to it, a drive to distill life's scattered moments into their essence. Fatherson seeks the center of the self, the nut in the shell. We have seen that father and son can be (and in reality are) mutual selfobjects to each other, but the strife to possess a scarce or unique selfhood is always an issue with Fatherson.

And yet, between jousts with one another, we fathers and sons yearn for the airy, horizonal, multiplex feminine, and not only to possess her. Years ago I wrote some verses on this. Here they are (somewhat dressed up for the occasion):

> Fecund and humble,
> Your sweetness shows purple
> Through skin that is white
> And mild as camellias.
>
> Orgasms boil my skin black
> Inside; an ape's mouth
> Tonguing blunt verbs
> Spews uncouthness in your air.
>
> Sometimes I wish I were girl too,
> Soft as a rabbit
> Aching tenderly in all my soft spots.

My "Beauty and the Beast," I suppose. In that fairy tale the Beast became beautiful, too (or "handsome," as we say of princes in the West), when he was transformed through Beauty's love into human form. It is a commonplace in our culture that love makes a man gentler and also more feminine. The young warriors of the ancient Aryan men's society (*mannerbund*) could not marry or love because their role was to fight, and to fight fiercely; their masculinity would diminish with too close an association to the feminine (Wikander 1938). Conversely, the bloody Beast became the mild prince through Beauty's love.

BEAUTY'S FATHER

As Bettelheim (1977) points out, "Beauty and the Beast" exemplifies the feminine oedipal complex in its most positive form. He seems
to regard the tale as the most successful of all in resolving a libidinal
conflict. Beauty's love for her father is translated into love for the
beast as she matures into womanhood.

> A child's Oedipal attachment to a parent is natural, desirable,
> and has the most positive consequences for all, if during the
> process of maturation it is transferred and transformed as it
> becomes detached from the parent and concentrated on the
> lover. Our Oedipal attachments . . . are the soil out of which
> permanent happiness grows if we experience the right evolu-
> tion and resolution of these feelings. (Bettelheim 1977, p. 307)

Sex loses its hideous face as it ceases to be incestuous, and is focused
on an appropriate partner. This happens with relatively little
trauma in "Beauty and the Beast." But the story is more complex
than this and contains also a Fatherson thread. Bettelheim retells
the story as follows.

A rich merchant, father of three daughters, loses his money.
He embarks on a trip to recover his fortune and asks his daughters
what he should bring them. The older two are greedy, but the youngest, Beauty, is modest and sweet. The two sisters ask for expensive
garments, while Beauty asks for nothing; only when pressed by her
father does she request a rose. The father becomes lost in the forest
but comes to a palace where he finds food and shelter but nobody
home. The next morning, the father sees a garden of beautiful roses
and gathers some for Beauty. As he does so, a frightful Beast appears and threatens to kill him as punishment for his theft. The
father begs for his life, telling the Beast that he wanted the flowers
for his daughter. The Beast relents, saying that if one of the daughters will take the father's place, he will let him go. If not, the father
must return in three months to die. As the father departs, the beast
gives him a chest filled with gold. The father comes home and gives
Beauty the roses; she insists on taking his place with the Beast.

At the Beast's castle, Beauty refuses to marry the Beast but
agrees that she will never leave him. However, she requests to visit
her father once more. The Beast agrees but tells Beauty that he will
die if she does not return within one week. She is tricked by her evil
sisters into overstaying her visit home, but in a dream she sees the

Beast on his death bed. She hurries back, and seeing the Beast near death from a broken heart realizes that she loves him. At this moment the Beast regains his true form as a prince, and they marry. The father, too, is happy.

The initial conflict in this story is not between Beauty and the Beast but between the Beast and Beauty's father. It is the father's theft of the Beast's roses which sets the main plot in motion, and the theft almost results in the father's untimely murder by the Beast. As Bettelheim notes, the roses represent Beauty's feminine nature; reversing this, we could say that Beauty embodies the feminine nature of the roses, which grow in the Beast's garden and are an image of his anima. After an initial struggle over ownership of the roses, the father exchanges his daughter for them—with her consent. One result is a bond of relationship between the father and his Beast son-in-law; a second result is the attainment of the feminine by both the Beast (who receives Beauty) and the father (who gains anima). Bettelheim recognizes a benefit to the father: "By transferring her original Oedipal love for her father to her future husband, Beauty gives her father the kind of affection most beneficial to him. This restores his failing health and provides him with a happy life in proximity to his beloved daughter" (1977, p. 308). I suggest that the father's gain is deeper, more psychological, than health and daughterly affection, important as these things are.

At the story's beginning, the father has lost all his money. It would appear that he is to undergo an initiation, of which the first step is this impoverishment, signifying ego abasement. In middle age, the father must let his ego go, along with his literal daughter, and in its and her place must find the anima. Like any old king, he must also leave his treasure and his kingdom to the son who will be king in his time. The latter, Fatherson theme is subtextual in "Beauty and the Beast," but we may suggest that the Beast is the father's true son and heir. There are literal sons in the story but, as Bettelheim notes, their role is insignificant.

The father's anima, beyond the roses which he gives to Beauty and his daughter herself, comes to him through the story as a whole and its effects on his psyche. It comes through his memory of the beautiful adventure, and especially of the events which occurred in the Beast's rose garden, where the psyches of the father and the unseen Beast each focused the same deep yet possessive love on the roses. In the story, and in memory, that love begins to transcend egos and shift towards unselfishness at the moment when the Beast realizes why the father wants the (already stolen) roses and gives them to him. It becomes completely unselfish when the father's "rose," Beauty, gives herself to the Beast with her father's glad consent.

We can spy a connection between anima and Fatherson here: it is the seeing-through and "relativizing" of each of their egos by anima which allows father and son to unite in Fatherson harmony. The love of each for the anima, and hers for them, is what makes the seeing-through possible, i.e., makes it possible for the Beast to become the prince, and the rich, masterful father of the story's beginning to become the dependent but beloved old father of its end. In terms of self psychology, the process is akin to what we described earlier, with the self becoming selfobject.

The hard and fast ego selves of father and son (-in-law) are made softer by their love for their anima, who is so selflessly devoted to them. It is the anima's apparently pure selfobjecthood, her lack of center, with which the self falls in love; developing under her tutelage beyond the brute desire to use her solely for its own ends, the self comes to love the anima for her very lack of focal (ego) selfhood and desires to be like her in this. In the very act of making the ego feel "special" by her willingness to be his selfobject, the anima undermines the ego's firm grip on himself and makes him yearn to be like her. But beyond this, father and son selves come to realize that *the anima herself also seeks "central" selfhood.*[1] They allow themselves to become selfobjects to her: the Beast lets Beauty leave, even at the cost of his own wasting away (fading) and thereby is transformed in her eyes into a prince; the father likewise gives Beauty away and fades into a happy old man. In this way strong male egos dissolve, freeing father and son for new ventures such as Fatherson union.

---

1. This is archetypal feminism, as in the tale of Sir Gawain and Dame Ragnell where the answer to the riddle "What does woman most desire?" is "to have sovereignty" (Zimmer, 1971: 90-95).

FATHERSON AND ANIMA IN *KING LEAR*

The same themes occur, but with a tragic end, in Shakespeare's *King Lear*. In this play, old King Lear attempts to hold onto his ego prerogatives with one hand while giving them away with the other. A common conflict within the Fatherson domain is here transposed into a father–daughter struggle, and the presence of the feminine in the son role gives *King Lear* its peculiar twist.

King Lear, growing older, decides to give his kingdom to his three daughters, Goneril, Regan, and Cordelia. He bases the decision of which portion to give each daughter on a vain contest in which the daughters are to vie with one another over how much each loves her father. Goneril and Regan pile on fulsome expressions of their devotion to him, but Cordelia is angered by her father's need for such a display and will not express an excessive love for him, pointing out that she must love her own husband equally. Accordingly (despite the appeal of his friend Kent), Lear gives his property to Goneril and Regan, leaving Cordelia nothing. All three daughters marry, and the older daughters' husbands (Cornwall and Albany) receive Lear's kingdom and, with their wives, proceed to abuse him. The dowerless Cordelia is married for love by the King of France and is out of the action for the next two acts.

In a parallel subplot, the Earl of Gloucester has two sons, Edgar and Edmund (a bastard). Just as Lear loves his faithless older daughters and is enraged by Cordelia's refusal to pledge her whole self to him, so Gloucester is taken in by the wily, deferential Edmund and ignores the genuine, but not servile, love of Edgar for him.

The tragedy unfolds as Lear tries to hold on to part of the kingdom he has given away by keeping one hundred knights as his own attendants. Goneril and Regan refuse to allow this and humiliate Lear in the process. His pride will not allow him to live dependent on either of them and Lear finds himself wandering unsheltered in a storm with his fool. Edmund, who hates both his legitimate brother and his father, finds a way to betray Edgar and Gloucester. Edgar feigns madness, and wanders in the wilderness with Lear; Gloucester is blinded and joins Lear and Edgar in their wanderings.

The main familial relationships in the drama are shown in the figure below.

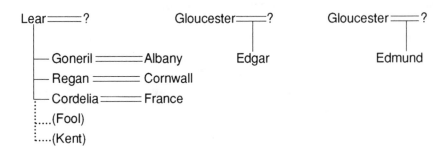

As the diagram makes clear, mothers are no part of the dramatist's concern: we are never introduced to Lear's wife (the mother of Goneril, Regan, and Cordelia) and likewise never learn even of the existence of Gloucester's wife or the identity of his paramour, the mother of Edmund. Father–daughter and father–son relationships are at the center of the work, intrapsychically as well as in outward reality.

Lear's developmental task is to let go of his kingship and to gain an anima connection through the only daughter capable of giving him this, Cordelia. He fails the test, in essence by trying to hold on to his daughters even as he is giving them (with the rest of his kingdom) away. This is the meaning of his demands for expressions of their love, and it is what Cordelia sees through in pointing out that a wife must also love her husband. We are in the realm of Levi-Strauss's "atom of kinship" again, with Lear attempting to unbalance the atom toward the father–daughter (similar to the brother–sister) side of the scale. Cordelia's task is to relativize Lear's ego, and her failure brings tragic consequences for himself and her. The humiliating dependency that Goneril and Regan try to force upon Lear is a travesty of the willing acceptance of age and passivity shown by Beauty's father. As the fool tells Lear, "they [Goneril and Regan] will make [you] an obedient father" (1.4.232). But a compensatory process is at work here, as the fool and Edgar (disguised as Tom O'Bedlam, a former inhabitant of the mental hospital) move an unwilling Lear closer to accepting his new state, and in the end he is reconciled to Cordelia (too late, alas, to save either of them).

Gloucester, at the same stage of life as Lear, likewise fails to let go his strong fatherly ego and give way to his sons. Instead, his wish to hold on beyond his time is projected onto his son Edgar: Gloucester is easily convinced by a letter Edmund has forged that Edgar is plotting his death. Edgar's supposed resentment of the father's grip on the life-substance is well expressed in this "letter":

> This policy and reverence of age makes the world bitter to our best of times, keeps our fortunes from us till our oldness cannot relish them. I begin to find an idle and fond bondage in the oppression of aged tyranny. . . . (*King Lear* 1.2.45-51)

Edmund then invents for Edgar, and "repeats" to Gloucester, the Fatherson philosophy that:

> sons at perfect age and fathers declined, the father should be as ward to the son, and the son manage his revenue. (1.2.74-76)

The irony, of course, is that these are Edmund's sentiments; *he* hates his father and covets his possessions, in part because Gloucester has humiliated him with his bastardy, but also because it is his nature to lust for power and hate whatever stands in his way.

Gloucester is mistaken as to the cause of the Fatherson rift but correct that it has taken place and speaks of "the bond cracked twixt son and father" (1.2.111-112). In fact, the story of *King Lear* is about the cracking of a number of familial bonds and the explosions resulting from this fission of the atom of kinship. In brief, Lear's bonds with his daughters are broken, as are those of his older daughters with their husbands and one another, as well as the sibling bond between Gloucester's sons. The conflagration leaves only Edgar and France actively alive of the main protagonists, although Goneril's husband Albany repents and is spared. In spite of the physical and psychic carnage, however, there is considerable psychological growth among the characters in the drama, and especially in Edgar, Gloucester, and Lear.

Perhaps in part because he has no sons, Lear's Father identification is rigid and unyielding. At the play's beginning, he is confronted with the reality of aging and responds impulsively and extremely by giving away his kingdom "while we unburdened crawl toward death" (1.1.40-41). This is a defensive act, an identification with the aggressor or turning passive into active: by giving his possessions away promptly, Lear hopes to avoid having them taken from him. His effort to retain his "hundred knights," as Regan and Goneril see, amounts to a denial of his passivity and old-age dependency. Although we are given no clue as to its etiology, the hatred for Lear by his older daughters is palpable from the beginning. As he resists their efforts to reduce him to powerless dependency, Regan and Goneril become positively murderous toward Lear and are pleased to let him go unprotected into the stormy night.

As it becomes clear that his daughters do not love him, and Lear realizes that he has lost their selfobject support, he also begins to lose the sense of who he is: "Does any know me? This is not Lear./ Does Lear walk thus, speak thus? Where are his eyes?/ Either his notion weakens, his discernings / are lethargied—Ha! Waking. 'Tis not so./ Who is it that can tell me who I am?" The fool answers, "Lear's shadow" (1.4.223-228).

Lear enters a liminal state in the wilderness and storm and matches the meteorological fury with his own howling rage.[2] Reduced almost to the status of a beast, Lear goes frankly mad, and through madness finally comes to his senses ("reason in madness" 4.6.175). The process of Lear's conversion is Dionysian and underworldly, and he takes his night journey in the company of "Old Tom" née Edgar, who is hiding in the disguise of a madman. Actually, it seems clear that Edgar is not just playacting and also undergoes a transformation, which renders him worthy to be the new king at the play's end.

King Lear's madness is, at least in part, a case of *hysteria,* which Hillman (1972) has shown to be a Dionysian disease. Thus Lear self-diagnoses: "O, how this mother swells up toward my heart! *Hysteria passio,* down thou climbing sorrow!" (2.4.55-56). Lear has an internal feminine organ, a "mother" (i.e., a womb), which pushes up toward his heart, making him mad but also "loosening" his rigid Father identity.[3]

---

2. The storm is itself an anima image (see Hillman 1985, p. 145).

3. Edgar also gains feminine qualities. Addressed by his father, Gloucester (who does not recognize him disguised as Tom O'Bedlam), "Now good sir, what are you?" Edgar replies: "A most poor man, made tame to fortune's blows, / Who, by the art of known and feeling sorrows, / Am *pregnant* to good pity . . . ." (4.6.223–226, my emphasis).

Lear's companion and teacher, Edgar, arrives naked and mouthing the words of a penitent or prophet; his self-knowledge seems to ignite Lear's own reflective capacity and, in a beautiful ecce homo, the once king contemplates Old Tom's and, by implication, his own human nature:

> Is man no more than this? Consider him well. Thou ow'st the worm no silk, the beast no hide, the sheep no wool, the cat no perfume. Ha! Here's three on's are sophisticated. Thou art the thing itself; unaccommodated man is no more but such a poor, bare, forked animal as thou art. (3.4.101-107)

Expressing solidarity with Old Tom, Lear tears off his own clothes and begins a folie à deux with his "philosopher" (4.3.175).

Together Old Tom and Lear enter an imaginative underworld of the "foul fiend" and his hordes of devilish minions, who include Flibbertigibbit, Smulkin, and Hoppedance. Old Tom has carried these demons in his body and knows them well; he is free to follow their promptings or not. Edgar's father, Gloucester, has come this way also, after having been blinded; he is suicidal and wants to leap from the cliffs of Dover. Edgar/Old Tom sees the demon behind his father's suicidal mood and helps his father to see it and to see beyond it to wisdom and faith. At this moment Lear achieves his apotheosis of madness and appears "fantastically dressed with wild flowers" (according to the stage directions). He orders Edgar "give the [pass] word"; in the same spirit Edgar answers, "sweet marjoram." One is reminded of the Dionysian wearing of garlands of leaves and flowers, of going naked, and of identification with beasts (Boer 1970, pp. 12, 14; Dodds 1966, p. 277).

Lear has gained some self-knowledge: he sees through his daughters' flattery and the self-assessment implied by the flattery: "They told me I was everything. Tis a lie: I am not ague-proof" (4.6.104-105). He also sees through some of his own projections: "Why dost thou lash that whore? Strip thine own back; Thou hotly lusts to use her in that kind For which thou whipp'st her" (4.6.161-163). Nevertheless, Lear's consciousness is partial and variable and will never be integrated, for the death of Cordelia (murdered by Edmund and Goneril) pushes him over the edge of the cliff, and he dies.

By showing us simultaneously a Fatherson drama without an explicit anima figure (that of Gloucester and sons), and one with a carrier of anima (that of Lear and his daughters and sons-in-law), Shakespeare gives a rich and full picture of the Fatherson and its ways of failure and fulfillment. For one thing, the Gloucester subplot makes it clearer that Lear's struggle is a Fatherson matter as well as an anima issue. Lear's sons-in-law are as cruel to him as his daughters, and we see their hatred for the old man on the same screen as Edmund's for his father. Most significant is that Edgar is a kind of "pueric" guru to Lear as to his own father Gloucester and becomes in effect Lear's true heir at the play's end.[4] The father–son bond between Edgar and Gloucester, and between Edgar and Lear, is made possible by the Dionysian/anima weakening of the egos of all three males.

It is in the Dionysian aspect of the play that the relativizing of fathers' and sons' egos by anima is most pronounced. Although the crux of *King Lear's* plot is Cordelia's refusal to flatter her father with the lie that he is "all" to her, her active anima role in the rest of the play is limited. After her departure for France, the feminine approaches Lear primarily through his hysteria, and in the overwhelming Nature that blows down his presumption of mastery. Edgar walks this road before Lear, who follows him and looks to him as a model. The feminine also occurs in untamed form in Goneril and Regan, whose hatred and lust is boundless and has the taste of a shadow maenad.

Lear's and Cordelia's last scene together, after they have been captured by Edmund, is a beautiful celebration of Lear's achievement of "being in anima" with his daughter. Lear comforts her with this fantasy of their shared life in captivity:

No, no, no, no! Come, let's away to prison.
We two will sing like birds i' the cage.
. . . So we'll live,
And pray, and sing, and tell old tales, and laugh
At gilded butterflies . . .
And take upon's the mystery of things,
As if we were God's spies; and we'll wear out,
In a walled prison, packs and sects of great ones,
That ebb and flow by the moon. (5.3.6-19)

---

4. See Collins (1991a) for more on the theme of the son as teacher and savior of the aging father.

Birds, butterflies, mystery, and the moon: Lear has worn out his rage and lust for mastery and has achieved a state of reflection. From this perspective, ego mastery (the "great ones") is seen as relative and fleeting and as subservient to the feminine rhythms of the moon. Lear himself has faded happily into the anima; he has gained "psychological femininity" (Hillman 1972).

King Lear thus gives us a beautiful image of Father transformed simultaneously through anima and through the puer/son. As in *Zen and the Art of Motorcycle Maintenance* (see chapter 1), the transformation happens in the wilderness, as "father" and "son" journey together far from places of ego mastery. In both works, madness and an underworld venture are necessary in order to relativize a senex ego. In common with "Beauty and the Beast," the anima in *Lear* inspires the father's ego to relax its pretensions of omnipotence and literal immortality and to become feminine.

King Lear also shows us anima scorned and vindictively bent on usurping the limelight occupied by a pretentious ego. Goneril and Regan flatter Lear that he is "all" while attempting to make him nothing and to take his all for themselves (actually each for herself, as becomes clear later in the play). Like Lady Macbeth, Lear's older daughters wear the pants in their families and scorn their husbands for being "milk livered" (4.2.51). But in classical Jungian terms, this is each daughter's *animus*. If they are Lear's negative anima figures, we have a case of the anima's animus.

A syzygy of anima and animus is achieved, at least momentarily, in the last lines of the play, as Edgar accepts his destiny to become the new king: "The weight of this sad time we must obey; Speak what we feel, not what we ought to say." He has gained feeling and will be a king whose acts are informed by a deep felt sense of himself, and not merely by what his ego tells him kings "ought" to be and do. Earlier, Edgar has prevailed in man-to-man combat with Oswald (sent to murder Gloucester) and with his brother Edmund, so apparently his newly gained psychological femininity has not diminished his prowess as a male.

Let us return explicitly to the theme of this chapter: the two kinds or aspects of consciousness represented by anima and Fatherson. Fatherson consciousness is centripetal while anima consciousness is centrifugal; anima is peripheral, Fatherson central. Yet Fatherson wants and needs the anima horizon and anima seeks the Fatherson's sovereignty at the center of things. The father's sacrifice of himself in giving way for his son has an anima dimension, and if he fails the sacrifice, the anima turned power-hungry witch may tear him to pieces and install herself—and her consort, his son—on father's throne.

This is one way of looking at the Indian tale of the "vampire" (*vetala*) and the king discussed in the introduction. In the story a king, indebted to a black magician who attempts to sacrifice him to the goddess Kali, is aided by a "vampire" enslaved by the power-seeking magician and so realizes in time what is afoot. The king turns the tables on the magician and decapitates him with Kali's sword. We can view this story as a case of a kingly ego (split into "good" and "bad" sides, represented by the king himself and the magician) who fails to pay the goddess her due, i.e., neglects his anima, and so loses his head to the goddess's aggressive, warrior side. The Hindu goddess often shows this dominant aspect, and is correspondingly often paired with a passive, supine, even dead consort.

We have primarily discussed the Fatherson's need for anima; the anima's need for central selfhood and craving for the Father's authority has only been touched upon. A fuller treatment of this topic is found in the feminist literature (Irigaray 1985) and I will make only a few more remarks on it.

In classical Jungian writing, the issue of the anima's search for personal power appears in discussions of the Great Mother's need for a son, or of the unconscious for consciousness. Much of the discussion is influenced by the ideas of Sir James Frazer and other nineteenth and early twentieth century anthropologists interested in matriarchy. The yearly death and renewal of the king, described in Frazer's *The Golden Bough* (1890-1915), implies that his function is to exercise sovereignty for the queen/mother, whose consort and victim he is; the king's periodic death reaffirms that ultimate sovereignty is hers and that he is only her organ, to be disposed of at and for her pleasure.[5] This matriarchal myth involves historical fantasy: a patriarchal system of society and consciousness is imagined to develop out of the matriarchal which, however, lives on in the social and psychological unconscious and continues to oppose the masculine usurper. The "return of the goddess" (Whitmont 1982) in contemporary, post-Christian society is a further working of the same fantasy.

---

5. Neumann characterizes the male, phallic principle as "the knife of the Great Goddess" and says that "the male remains inferior to, and at the mercy of, the Feminine" (1955, p. 303).

CHAPTER 5

The Failed Father
Old Reprobates and Their Sons

Setting right what has been spoiled by the
father. If there is a son, no blame adheres to
the departed father.

I Ching, *Hexagram 18*

Old men are not always wise or venerable. From a feminine perspective, "dirty old men" are the object of a special ridicule, and the
mythology of the middle-aged man as failure or loser in his children's
eyes motivates American literary works such as *Death of a Sales-
man.* The issue is particularly charged for males. If failed fathers
are often risible to their daughters, they are a source of profound
shame to themselves and to their sons, shame which can sometimes
be redeemed in comedy but more often leads to violence. The inadequate, failed, ridiculous father: Dad as clown. We will explore this
painful topic—at once embarrassing and shamefully pleasurable to
sons—through two nineteenth-century literary classics from Russia and the United States, *The Brothers Karamazov* and *Huckleberry Finn.* The reprobate Father—the inverse of tyrant or demon—
is a variation on the oedipal theme which causes a similar shift toward the picaresque in the character of the son-heroes of these novels.

We are not used to finding comedy in Dostoevsky, although
one may think of Woody Allen films where the filmmaker's nebbish
persona lends itself a ridiculous dignity by comparing his petty
troubles with a Dostoevskian standard. Violence, of course, and especially father-son violence, is everywhere in Dostoevsky's work. It
is therefore at first surprising to find the latest translators of *The
Brothers Karamazov* saying that the novel is essentially "comic"
(Pevear and Volokhonsky 1990, p. xvii). What could be comic in the
story of a (bastard) son's murder of his father and the false impris-
onment of another son for the crime?

To move to another continent and ostensibly another genre;
Mark Twain's *Adventures of Huckleberry Finn* (1965) is an acknowledged comic masterpiece, but at its center is the attempted murder
of a son by a father whose dead and bloated corpse the son later
comes upon (without knowing its identity) in a house drifting on the

flooded Mississippi river. How is this comic? In both novels, although with more success in *Karamazov,* a reprobate father is at the motivational heart of the action, setting in motion his sons' quest for initiation and manhood. Dostoevsky and Mark Twain work to come to terms with the rogue father by poking fun at the old bastard; Dostoevsky goes further and uncovers in the shameful, sardonic father the germ of a homeopathic cure for his wretchedness and that of his sons.

HUCK'S PAP
IDENTIFYING WITH THE REPROBATE

Huckleberry Finn begins where *The Adventures of Tom Sawyer* left off, with the former outcaste Huck living in town with the Widow Douglas and her sister Miss Watson, who are trying to "sivilize" him. He and Tom have split the $12,000 treasure they found in the robbers' cave, so Huck is now a person of property and more acceptable to the "quality." His father, "pap," has disappeared but returns near the beginning of the book and interrupts Huck's unwilling journey toward respectability. Pap is a shameful pig of a man and is in fact often compared to a hog. Thus, Tom Sawyer says that pap "used to lay drunk with the hogs in the tanyard" (p. 9). Huck describes pap on his return as follows:

> He was most fifty, and he looked it. His hair was long and tangled and greasy, and hung down, and you could see his eyes shining through like he was behind vines. It was all black, no gray; so was his long, mixed-up whiskers. There warn't no color in his face, where his face showed; it was white; not like another man's white, but a white to make a body sick, a white to make a body's flesh crawl—a tree-toad white, a fish-belly white. As for his clothes—just rags, that was all. He had one ankle resting on t'other knee, the boot on that foot was busted, and two of his toes stuck through, and he worked them now and then. His hat was laying on the floor—an old black slouch with the top caved in, like a lid.

Pap knows that he is trash and deeply resents the shameful fact. Most of all he resents that his son is becoming "better" than he, and he exerts himself to get hold of Huck's $6,000 and take the boy away from the widow and her sister, to return him to the hog's life into which he was born. As pap says:

I'll learn people to bring up a boy to put on airs over his own father and let on to be better'n what he is. . . . Your mother couldn't read, and she couldn't write, nuther, before she died. None of the family couldn't before they died. I can't; and here you're a-swelling yourself up like this. I ain't the man to stand it—you hear? (p. 20)

Pap goes on, a little later:

Ain't you a sweet-scented dandy, though? A bed; and bed-clothes; and a look'n'-glass; and a piece of carpet on the floor—and your own father got to sleep with the hogs in the tanyard. I never see such a son. I bet I'll take some of these frills out o' you before I'm done with you. Why, there ain't no end to your airs—they say you're rich. Hey?—how's that? (p. 21)

Pap's shame and envy pour out during the time he and Huck live together in a cabin in the Illinois woods. Pap obsesses about a free "nigger" who has a white shirt, shiny hat, gold watch and silver-headed cane and compares his own degradation to the nigger's ex-alted state. He fumes that the man should be "put up at auction" and complains at "the cool way of that nigger—why, he wouldn't 'a' give me the road if I hadn't shoved him out o' the way" (p. 27).

Pap wins a custody battle for Huck, convincing a judge who doesn't know him that he wants to reform himself. The judge takes pap into his own home, dresses him in clean clothes, and lectures him on temperance. Pap is filled with emotion at being treated so well and holds out his hand to the judge and his family, saying:

Look at it, gentlemen and ladies all; take a-hold of it; shake it. There's a hand that was the hand of a hog; but it ain't so no more; it's the hand of a man that's started in on a new life, and'll die before he'll go back. . . .It's a clean hand now; shake it—don't be afeard. (p. 23)

Pap's newfound resolution lasts only a few hours, of course; he gets drunk that night on the judge's money and falls out the window. After a period of drinking, carousing, and being jailed, pap seizes Huck and takes him across the Mississippi River to Illinois where they live the old life of relaxed squalor, "lazy and jolly, laying off comfortable all day, smoking and fishing, and no books nor study" (p. 24). Soon Huck "didn't want to go back no more" and says "it was

pretty good times up in the woods there, take it all around." But
pap's drinking leads to physical abuse of the boy ("pap got too handy
with his hick'ry"), and Huck decides to escape.

It is striking that Huck has none of pap's shame or much
overt feeling of any sort toward his father; he is merely "comfortable" with pap's absence at the book's beginning and describes the
old man's degradation with a dry amusement that only adds to its
horror; but the expectable emotions of a boy toward this disastrous
father—rage, low self-esteem, shame, sense of loss, self-blame, fantasies of closeness—are missing. Even when pap is revealed at the
novel's end to be dead, Huck shows no emotion. In fact, Huck's feelings toward pap seem to have gone underground, into the boy's unconscious, and his shameful and ashamed father metamorphoses in
the book's pivotal sequence into a figure of death for Huck, who
also—in a bitter Fatherson irony—himself appears to his drunken
pap as Death personified.[1] Pap drinks himself to the point of the
DT's after locking himself and Huck into the cabin. The old man
passes out and Huck falls asleep. Then:

> I don't know how long I was asleep, but all of a sudden there
> was an awful scream and I was up. There was pap looking wild,
> and skipping around every which way and yelling about
> snakes. He said they was crawling up his legs. . . .By and by he
> raised up part way and listened, with his head to one side. He
> says, very low:
>
> "Tramp—tramp—tramp; that's the dead; tramp—tramp—
> tramp; they're coming after me; but I won't go. Oh, they're here!
> don't touch me—don't! Hands off—they're cold; let go. Oh, let a
> poor devil alone!"
>
> By and by he rolled out and jumped up on his feet looking
> wild, and he see me and went for me. He chased me round and
> round the place with a clasp-knife, calling me the Angel of
> Death, and saying he would kill me, and then I couldn't come
> for him no more. (p. 29)

---

1. Alfred Kazin calls this sequence "crucial" in his Afterword to the Ban-
tam edition of *Huckleberry Finn* cited here (Twain 1884, p. 289).

I suspect that Huck is pap's Angel of Death because the old man's shame is centered on his son and because his life cannot be redeemed by a son who he envies so venomously. He must kill Huck to stop the serpents of his own self-hatred, envy, and shame from devouring him. In the Vedic Indian story of Sunahsepa, discussed in the introduction, we read that the son is the father's road "to the far shore of death." In *Huckleberry Finn,* the road is broken (as it is for father characters in the Indian story as well), and the son becomes the *agent* of death for the father, who then attempts to turn passive into active by murdering the son (in "Sunahsepa" this is the figure of Ajigarta). Reading all this as occurring in Huck's unconscious— legitimate in terms of Freudian or Jungian depth psychology, if totally foreign to the self-consciousness of our text—we would have a murderous envy from the father complex attacking the ego (or self) of the boy, who also desires to kill it both for the sake of self protection and to eliminate a source of intense, if denied, shame.[2] Rather than a mutually supportive father and son acting as selfobjects to one another, we have father and son seeking to destroy one another in order to survive, which requires that each be rid of the shame of his Fatherson other.

Huck escapes his crazed father by faking his own murder (significantly with the blood of a wild pig), and goes down river with Miss Watson's escaped slave, Jim. In their riverine odyssey, Jim and Huck encounter a rogues' gallery of proud and ashamed men who attempt to inflate their own self-sense at the expense of others. Among the stops on this narcissistic tour, consider the feud of the Sheperdsons and the Grangerfords, and the murder of the boastful Boggs by Col. Sherburn. Pride and slights to reputation and sense of self move the aristocratic egos of these men (it is always men) to murder the enemy who is responsible for the slight. Huck is taken in by the Grangerfords (as by other families along the river) and has time to form attachments to them. When two Grangerford boys near

---

2. In a "Notice" placed by Mark Twain at the front of the book, the author tries to fend off interpretations of his work: "Persons attempting to find a motive in this narrative will be prosecuted; persons attempting to find a moral in it will be banished; persons attempting to find a plot in it will be shot." Does Twain protest too much because he senses that tacit meanings—meanings that might be too close for comfort—lurk near the surface of his text?

his own age—one had become his friend—are murdered, Huck for
once owns the intense feelings that must also be present but unex-
pressed toward his father:

> All of a sudden, bang! bang! bang! goes three or four guns . . .
> The boys jumped for the river—both of them hurt—and as they
> swum down the current the men along the bank shooting at
> them and singing out "Kill them, kill them!" It made me so sick
> I almost fell out of the tree. I ain't a-going to tell all that hap-
> pened—it would make me sick again if I was to do that. I
> wished I hadn't ever come ashore that night to see such things.
> I ain't ever going to get shut of them—lots of times I dream
> about them . . . .
> I reckoned I was to blame somehow . . . .
> When I got down out of the tree I crept along down the
> riverbank a piece, and found the two bodies laying in the edge
> of the water, and tugged at them till I got them ashore; then I
> covered up their faces, and got away as quick as I could. I cried
> a little when I was covering up Buck's face, for he was mighty
> good to me. (pp. 111–112)

Huck is capable of forming friendships with peers and seems
on the verge of normal heterosexuality (although he would be stifled
by married life and seems destined to be a wanderer). But there is
no suggestion that Huck has ever deeply identified with an adult
male or could do so. His friendship with Jim does not contradict
this: Jim is viewed through the glass of slavery as a superstitious
child rather than as a man. Instead of idealizing potential father
figures, Huck sees through their pretense (e.g. the Duke and the
Dauphin/King). But Huck does not show the classic oedipal hatred
of the father; instead, he is cool and dispassionate and expresses his
anger through a dry, observant wit. Furthermore, Huck seems to
have no narcissism: he is neither proud nor ashamed. Like a wooden
ball among magnets, Huck seems to pass through the fields of passionate self-concern characteristic of the men of his society without
injury or involvement, although he shows feelings toward women
and children and is a good friend to young men of his age. At the end
of the book, Huck is ready to "light out for the territory," again es-
caping the efforts of the womenfolk to "sivilize" him. We have confidence that he will succeed out there, although—or because—he is,
at least on the surface, a Fatherson "neuter."

FOUR BROTHERS IN QUEST OF A FATHER
THE KARAMAZOV SONS

The Brothers Karamazov is about a father and his four sons, three legitimate (by two mothers) and one a bastard. The bastard, Smerdyakov, is never openly acknowledged as a son and lives as his father's servant, yet his character and actions are those of a (negative) son. In his exquisite shame and (implicit) hatred for the father, he strongly resembles Edmund in *King Lear*. The self-sense and esteem of all four sons has been deeply injured by the repugnant character and abusive actions of their appalling father, and the narrative follows the sons' efforts to work through the failed Fatherson dynamic as each is caught in it. The image of the ridiculous, inept father, and efforts to redeem him, are central for the Karamazovs and also form the underlying motivational heart of the novel as a whole. It is this utterly serious work with the buffoon father that explains why *Karamazov* is, in the words of its translators, a comedy of "manner" (p. xi).

The father, whom I will call simply Karamazov, is acknowledged by everyone to be a miserable human being and a neglectful and hateful father. He is also, like pap Finn, physically loathsome:

> I have already mentioned that he had grown very bloated. His physiognomy by that time presented something that testified acutely to the characteristics and essence of his whole life. Besides the long, fleshy bags under his eternally insolent, suspicious and leering little eyes, besides the multitude of deep wrinkles on his fat little face, a big Adam's apple, fleshy and oblong like a purse, hung below his sharp chin, giving him a sort of repulsively sensual appearance. Add to that a long, carnivorous mouth with plump lips, behind which could be seen the little stumps of black, almost decayed teeth." (p. 23)

He is preoccupied with his sense of his own absurdity and worries it like a hurting tooth. Karamazov has made a career of owning and being the first to observe his essential foolishness and often and eagerly expresses it, as when he tells the holy elder Zosima, "I'm a buffoon out of shame" (p. 43). A little later Karamazov suggests that his lack of self-worth results from Fatherson defects: "I am a lie and the father of a lie! Or maybe not the father of a lie, I always get the texts mixed up; let's say the son of a lie. . ." (p. 44). In his audience with Father Zosima, Karamazov behaves like a prospective analysand desperately in search of a fatherly therapist and lets spill a pitiful farrago of confession, partial insight, and self-justification. When Zosima, perceiving his character, tells him to "Be at ease, and feel completely at home. And above all do not be so ashamed of yourself," Karamazov answers:

> Completely at home? You mean in my natural state? Oh, that is much, too much—but I'm touched. . . .That remark you just made "Not to be so ashamed of myself, for that is the cause of everything"—it's as if you pierced me right through and read inside me. That is exactly how it all seems to me, when I walk into a room, that I'm lower than anyone else, and that everyone takes me for a buffoon, so "Why not, indeed, play the buffoon, I'm not afraid of your opinions, because you're all, to a man, lower than me!" That's why I'm a buffoon, I'm a buffoon out of shame, great elder, out of shame. (p. 43)

The kindly and accurate mirroring responses of the elder touch Karamazov momentarily, but as an "old liar" who has been "play-acting all [his] life" (p. 73), he cannot sustain the moment and reverts to his pose of the innocent, unfairly injured fool. It is his oldest son Dmitri whom Karamazov hates most and claims to have been most injured by. And, in fact, this father and son do cause one another exquisite pain.

Father Karamazov neglected all three of his legitimate sons, letting them be raised by others and showing almost no interest in them. The novel depicts the encounter between the sons, now grown to young men, and their father, who cannot any more ignore their existence although contact with them painfully stimulates his sense of shame. Dmitri has attended military school and lived the fast, dissolute life of a bachelor officer, freely spending money obtained from his father as an advance on his birthright. The old man, who envies his vigorous son, is also stung by Dmitri's contempt for him and has deceived him into thinking that he has more coming than is in fact due. After four years of advancing him money, he gleefully reveals that Dmitri is penniless. Dmitri is enraged with his father and becomes even more furious when the old man offers money to a young courtesan, Grushenka, with whom Dmitri has fallen in love. It is this quasi-oedipal triangle that apparently motivates the murder of Karamazov, for which Dmitri is falsely convicted and sentenced to Siberia.

Ivan, the second son, and his younger brother, Alyosha (Karamazov's two children by his second wife), were likewise abandoned by their father but seem to have had somewhat more adequate parenting than Dmitri. Ivan is a gifted writer and thinker but struggles with issues of faith and doubt and poses, at different times, as an ardent champion of the church and as a confident atheist. Like Dmitri (and their father), he suffers from an almost complete inability to idealize. Alyosha is Ivan's contrary: he becomes the disciple of a holy man—the elder Zosima—who he passionately reveres and through this idealization of a truly good man achieves the ability to mirror others without judging them. In turn, he can be idealized by others. Because Alyosha is loved by everyone, he becomes the empathic messenger who passes Hermes-like into the lives and hearts of all the major characters of the novel and communicates them to others without himself being tainted by their ignoble passions. Thus, Alyosha makes the novel move, and *Karamazov* is, in a way, as Dostoevsky claimed, his book. Alyosha alone does not believe that his father is "just a buffoon" (p. 133).

Karamazov's three legitimate children were abandoned, I speculate, because the very existence of sons was implicitly felt as a reproach by their deeply ashamed father, who anticipated their contempt for him. His relationship with them as adults—excepting Alyosha—aims to make them as depraved and contemptible as he is. As in *Huckleberry Finn,* the metaphor of the pig appears in Father Karamazov's self-image. During an alcoholic evening with Ivan and Alyosha (who does not drink), the old man addresses Ivan: "What are you staring at me for? What kind of look is that? Your eyes look at me and say 'You drunken pig!'" A little later he speaks to both boys: "Ah you children, my babes, my little piglets. . ." (p. 136). It is not only his sons who Karamazov tries to lower to his level; he also makes up stories that depict the elder Zosima himself as a charlatan and rogue who does not believe in God and uses his office to steal money and indulge his "sensuality" (p. 135).

With Smerdyakov, his illegitimate son, Karamazov can act with fewer constraints and in fact has lowered the boy to the status of servant and cook. Smerdyakov was raised in Karamazov's household by the depressive and dull-witted servant Grigory and is a moral monster: psychopathically arrogant and contemptuous of others, as a boy he was fond of "hanging cats and then burying them with ceremony." As a young man, Smerdyakov is casually ridiculed and abused by his father, who tolerates his uncouth presence for the pleasure of baiting him, for his casuistical refutations of Christianity, and for his excellent cabbage pies.

Smerdyakov's mother was a village idiot, a "holy fool," who died at twenty giving birth to Smerdyakov in Karamazov's garden. Although denying that he is the father of her child, Karamazov makes it clear that he fancied the unwashed creature—known as "Stinking Lizaveta"—and that "For me, there's no such thing as an ugly woman." He elaborates: "The barefoot or ugly ones have to be taken by surprise . . . so that they're enraptured, smitten, ashamed that such a gentleman should have fallen in love with such a grimy creature" (p. 136). Smerdyakov does not often express his anger and shame at his parentage, but in one revealing scene he tells a young woman with whom he is flirting, "I'd have killed a man in a duel with a pistol for calling me low-born, because I came from Stinking Lizaveta without a father" (p. 224). He also lets it slip that he hates Karamazov and all his sons, who he refers to as "madmen" (p. 225). Smerdyakov says that Ivan "made reference to me that I'm a stinking lackey" and that "Dmitri is worse than any lackey, in his behavior, in his intelligence, and in his poverty" (p. 225). Ivan—who is, of the three legitimate sons, the most similar to Smerdyakov—at first finds the "lackey" fascinating, but then notices that "a boundless vanity began to appear and betray itself, an injured vanity besides" (p. 266).

Smerdyakov wants to leave his lackey's life and move to Moscow, where he thinks his skills in cooking French *specialités* will make his fortune. It is clearly implied in the text that he killed Karamazov both because he hated him and in order to steal the 3,000 rubles which the old man had prepared to give to Grushenka if she came to him; the money would allow Smerdyakov to open his restaurant.

Karamazov is filled with variations on the theme of ridiculous and otherwise unidealizable fathers. In fact, almost all of the action is motivated by the quest to idealize or to cope with the inability to do so. It is easy to see that Alyosha's relationship to the elder Zosima is one of idealization, but I would claim that in close counterpoint to it must be placed Ivan's relationships in fantasy to his "Grand Inquisitor" and "devil." Further, Dmitri's exquisite shame and shaky pride rest on the sandy foundation of his father's lack of idealizability. We will look at each son separately and also examine the heartbreaking subplot of the doomed boy Ilyusha and his absurd but beloved father.

IVAN

In the most famous segment of the novel, "The Grand Inquisitor," Ivan recites to Alyosha a story, which he says he wrote in younger days, about a second coming of Jesus during the Spanish Inquisition. After the Lord performs miracles (He raises a child from the dead, etc.), an old Inquisitor has Him arrested and intends to burn Him at the stake for "interfering" in the Church's hard-won control over human freedom. At bottom, the story is about the Inquisitor's (i.e., the Church's) inability to idealize Christ, and the Church's subsequent fall into the negative senex and power lust. As Alyosha says "Your Inquisitor doesn't believe in God, that's his whole secret!" (p. 261). The Inquisitor is an accomplished canon lawyer and makes a strong case against Christ, accusing the Lord in his cell of overestimating men: He promised heavenly bread, but men seek only the earthly sort; He preached freedom but men need to obey. The old man tells Christ the carefully concealed truth about the Church's work: "I do not want your love, for I do not love you . . . . For a long time now we have not been with you, but with him [i.e., Satan] . . . we took from him what you so indignantly rejected, that last gift he offered you when he showed you all the kingdoms of the earth: we took Rome and the sword of Caesar from him, and proclaimed ourselves sole rulers of the earth. . ." (p. 257).

Christ as Father overestimated men, his sons, by asking them to live in recognition of their eternal relationship with Him, freely acknowledged without the reinforcement of worldly nurturance, power, or certainty. What men want, however, and are capable of is only to seek to fill their bellies and to obey authority. The old Inquisitor is bitterly aware of his own failure to live up to Christ's demands and hates Him for making them. This is a true Fatherson conundrum: the son cannot idealize the father because he cannot live up to the father's idealized view of him. Hatred rises from failure to be what father demands and leads to efforts to bring the father down. The proud old Inquisitor would burn Christ in order to deidealize Him and so relieve his own sense of unworthiness. At the end of his monologue, however, Christ approaches the Inquisitor and kisses him on the lips; after this, the old man cannot burn his

Lord and realizes that he still loves and idealizes Him, even though his sense of his own failure remains. He opens the door and tells Christ to "Go and do not come again . . ." (p. 262).

Because he cannot accept Christ or the Church as idealizable father images, let alone his natural father, Ivan has little ability to see himself as a father, or to father others. What he sees are the abuses of fathers (and mothers) toward their children, and he has collected a number of choice examples of fatherly cruelty. Yet Ivan hopes for disproof of what he sees with his own eyes and compares this longed-for, irrational shift of perspective to a non-Euclidian geometry which will transcend the Euclidian world in which we live: a world where seven-year-old girls are beaten savagely and self-righteously by their birch-wielding parents (p. 241). In the end, however, Ivan—like the Inquisitor—confesses that he does have faith in spite of the absurdity of God's cruel fatherhood. His faith comes from archetypal sources but is elicited by Alyosha, who imitates Christ and kisses Ivan on the lips as they part. Ivan's position, at least in the first half of the book, can be summarized in his own words: "It's not that I don't accept God, Alyosha, I just most respectfully return him the ticket" (an allusion to a Schiller poem, suggesting refusal to pay the price of "admission" to God's world, if this includes the suffering of a child).

ALYOSHA

As in many fairy tales, the youngest brother of the three is the wisest and best, and in the end proves to be the salvation of his elders. But Alyosha, clearly the best of the Karamazovs, must first pass a test in which he is tempted to deny and deidealize his guru, the elder Zosima. Dostoevsky gives us considerable history and lore surrounding the institution of "elders" and notes that by tradition the bodies of holy saints do not decay after death. In Father Zosima's monastery, this was true within living memory of two elders. It was widely recalled of one of these that "not only was there no odor from the late elder Varsonofy, but he even exuded a fragrance." Hence, the expectation was that Father Zosima's body, after he died, would not decay but instead produce miracles; consequently, the windows in the room where his body was laid need not be opened. When Zosima's body began to stink, the faith of many who had revered him also decayed. "Above all, there was envy of the dead man's holiness . . . . That is why I think that many, having noticed the odor of corruption coming from his body . . . were immensely pleased" (p. 331). The elder's ascetic rival, Father Ferapont, was particularly glad and "thundered" in an exorcistic fury, " 'The deceased, your saint here,' he turned to the crowd pointing at the coffin with his finger, 'denied devils. He gave purgatives against devils. So they've bred like spiders in the corners. And on this day he got himself stunk. In this we see a great sign from God' " (p. 335). Ferapont reveals a little later the envy of Father Zosima which underlay his gleeful rage: "Tomorrow they will sing 'My Helper and Defender' over him—a glorious canon—and over me when I croak just 'What Earthly Joy'—a little song . . ." (p. 336).

Alyosha, like the others, had been expecting miracles. Although not embarrassed for himself by the elder's humiliation (ashamed of his gullibility), he is empathically chagrined that "he who. . .was to have been exalted higher than anyone in the whole world. . .instead of receiving the glory that was due him, was suddenly thrown down and disgraced! Why? Who had decreed it?" Baited by his cynical friend Rakitin—one of those pleased by the elder's fall—Alyosha echoes Ivan's theodicy: "I do not rebel against my God, I simply 'do not accept his world'" (p. 341). But at this nadir of Alyosha's spirit, fate—and Rakitin's desire to bring him still lower—intervene. Rakitin takes Alyosha to Grushenka's; unknown to Rakitin (who she has bribed to bring Alyosha to her, so that she can "eat him up") this "evil" woman is herself at a liminal moment. An old love, her "officer," is calling her after five years' abandonment, and she is preparing to go to him; instead of "eating" him, she opens her heart to Alyosha, who is able to help and "forgive" her. This encounter with Grushenka becomes the miracle Alyosha has waited for, but he sees now for the first time that the elder's healing powers must be mediated by his—Alyosha's—own action.

Returning to the monastery, Alyosha has a vision of Father Zosima present at Christ's first miracle, when He turned water into wine at the wedding in Cana. The elder teaches Alyosha that he—and Alyosha—are present at Christ's miracle because they have given, through their deeds, the "new wine" of faith in God's world to others. He declares the end of Alyosha's time of initiation and sets him on his path: "Begin, my dear, begin, my meek one, to do your work!" (p. 361). Alyosha leaves the monastery ecstatic, and in one of the great moments in fiction he accepts God's world. His senses are heightened, and we feel with him the sky and earth encompassed in the universal, all-mirroring love which Alyosha realizes.

Filled with rapture, his soul yearned for freedom, space, vastness. Over him the heavenly dome, full of quiet, shining stars,
hung boundlessly. From the zenith to the horizon the still-dim
Milky Way stretched its double strand. Night, fresh and quiet,
almost unstirring, enveloped the earth. The white towers and
golden domes of the church gleamed in the sapphire sky. The
luxuriant autumn flowers in the flower beds near the house
had fallen asleep until morning. The silence of the earth
merged with the silence of the heavens, the mystery of the earth
touched the mystery of the stars . . . Alyosha stood gazing and
suddenly, as if he had been cut down, threw himself to the
earth.

He did not know why he was embracing it, he did not try to
understand why he longed so irresistibly to kiss it, to kiss all of
it, but he was kissing it, weeping, sobbing, and watering it with
his tears, and he vowed ecstatically to love it, to love it unto
ages of ages. . . .But with each moment he felt clearly something as firm and immovable as this heavenly vault descend
into his soul. Some sort of idea, as it were, was coming to reign
in his mind—now for the whole of his life and unto all ages of
ages. He fell to the earth a weak youth and rose up a fighter,
steadfast for the rest of his life, and he knew it and felt it suddenly, in that very moment of his ecstasy." (pp. 362-363)

Alyosha is a man now, a true because *initiated* man. He has
become deeply one with his Father and is of his company. But
Alyosha does not lose his boyish innocence and partly for this reason can be idealized by boys in another ecstatic passage at the end of
the novel. As an authentic man who has not lost touch with his
inner child, Alyosha can inspire faith and hope in a group of boys
after the funeral of their dead companion Ilyusha.

DMITRI

The oldest of the acknowledged brothers is, as I noted earlier, the
most obviously damaged. For the first half of the novel, Dmitri is
consumed "with the ugliness and horror of his struggle with his own
father for this woman" (p. 365). The second half deals with his trial
for the father's murder, his "soul's journey through torments" (the
title of chapter 3.9.3), through which he will be redeemed and—in a
way—initiated. While in custody and on trial, Dmitri is subjected to
the questioning of the police and prosecutor, but the transformative

questioning is also internal. Dmitri looks into his own heart's darkness and begins for the first time to gain consciousness of his relation to his father and the Fatherson. As he tells his questioners :

> "You see, gentlemen, I did not like his appearance, it was somehow dishonorable, boastful, trampling on all that's holy, mockery and unbelief, loathsome, loathsome! But now he's dead I think differently."
> "I'm sorry that I hated him so much."
> "I'm not good myself, gentlemen, that's the thing, I'm not so beautiful myself and therefore I had no right to consider him repulsive . . . ." (p. 462)

Dmitri realizes that his life has been an abortive quest for "nobility," the opposite of the "loathsome mockery" of the good which he had seen as his father's nature.

> This is precisely what has tormented me all my life, that I thirsted for nobility, that I was, so to speak, a sufferer for nobility, seeking it with a lantern, Diogenes lantern, and meanwhile all my life I've been doing only dirty things . . . . (p. 462)

Dmitri's dirtiest, most shameful secret, confessed to his inquisitors during a long night's interrogation, is that he stole 3,000 rubles from the upper-class woman, Katerina (Katya) Ivanovna, with whom he had been in love before he met Grushenka. Katerina had asked Dmitri to send the money to a relative in Moscow, but Dmitri instead spent half of it entertaining Grushenka at an inn during their only night together and kept the remaining 1,500 in an amulet around his neck. When Grushenka went to her "officer," Dmitri decided to kill himself, after another night of debauchery at the inn—paid for with the remainder of Katya's money. Dmitri is arrested during the second half of this night and before morning endures an extraordinary ordeal of laying and being laid bare. Stripped of defenses, Dmitri's self-esteem is flayed and peeled away, and his face is rubbed in his own baseness and ignobility. The dark night ends with the beginning of Dmitri's transformation, which takes place in a dream parallel to Alyosha's vision and Ivan's "Inquisitor."

> It seemed he was driving somewhere in the steppe, in a place where he had served once long ago; he is being driven through the slush by a peasant, in a cart with a pair of horses. And it

seems to Mitya that he is cold, it is the beginning of November,
and snow is pouring down in big, wet flakes that melt as soon
as they touch the ground . . . . And there is a village nearby—
black, black huts, and half of the huts are burnt, just charred
beams sticking up. And at the edge of the village there are peas-
ant women standing along the road, many women, a long line
of them, all of them thin, wasted, their faces a sort of brown
color. Especially that one at the end—such a bony one, tall,
looking as if she were forty, but she may be only twenty, with a
long, thin face, and in her arms a baby is crying, and her breasts
must be all dried up, not a drop of milk in them. And the baby
is crying, crying, reaching out its bare little arms, its little fists
somehow all blue from the cold.

"Why are they crying? Why are they crying?" Mitya asks . . .

"The wee one," the driver answers, "it's the wee one crying."

"But why is it crying?" Mitya insists . . . "why are its little
arms bare, why don't they wrap it up?"

"The wee one's cold, its clothes are frozen, they don't keep
it warm."

"But why is it so? Why?" foolish Mitya will not leave off . . . .

And he feels within himself that, though his questions have
no reason or sense, he still certainly wants to ask in just that
way, and he should ask in just that way. And he feels a tender-
ness such as he has never known before surging up in his heart,
he wants to weep, he wants to do something for them all, so
that the wee one will no longer cry . . . . (pp. 507–508)

Dmitri wakes from this dream strengthened and readier to face the
ordeals that still await him. He has taken a first step toward his
own fatherhood and feels himself, for the first time in his life, at
peace within the Fatherson, as a potential father to the "wee one."

ILYUSHA

Much of the second half of *The Brothers Karamazov* deals with the
life and death of the nine-year-old boy Ilyusha Snegiryov and with
his family and friends. Ilyusha's father is a failed officer who is
taunted by schoolboys and called "whiskbroom" because of his thin
red beard. He is a "buffoon" and "clown" out of shame, like Huck's
pap and old Karamazov, but benign and sympathetic. Ilyusha passionately defends his ridiculous father and, in fact, has stabbed an
older boy, Kolya Krasotkin, in the thigh for calling him "whiskbroom." Earlier in the novel, Dmitri had humiliated Snegiryov by

challenging him to a duel and dragging him about by his beard. Evidently Dmitri found his own shadow in this fellow officer, who like him struggles to maintain dignity and a sense of honor in squalid circumstances caused by his own gambling and alcoholism. Snegiryov is held in contempt by his wife and daughters, who he shames by his clowning and absurd swings between vanity and self-depreciation. Only his boy upholds the father's honor, and it is only his pride in his son that sustains Snegiryov. As he boasts to Alyosha:

> "Allow me to explain the story more particularly. The thing is that after the event [when Dmitri dragged him by the beard] all the children at school began calling him whiskbroom . . . They began teasing him, and a noble spirit arose in Ilyusha. An ordinary boy, a weak son, would have given in, would have felt ashamed of his father, but this one stood up for his father, alone against everyone." (p. 205)

But Ilyusha has humiliated himself to save his father. When Dmitri challenged Snegiryov to a duel, Ilyusha begged him to "Let go, let go, it's my Papa, my Papa, forgive him" and kissed Dmitri's hand (p. 204). This degradation "crushed" Ilyusha and further wounded his pride in his father.

> "Papa, the way he treated you, papa!" "It can't be helped, Ilyusha," I said. "Don't make peace with him, papa, don't make peace. The boys say he gave you ten rubles for it." "No, Ilyusha," I said, "I won't take any money from him, not for anything." Then he started shaking all over, seized my hand in both his hands, and kissed it again. "Papa," he said, "papa, challenge him to a duel; they tease me at school, they say you're a coward and won't challenge him to a duel, but you'll take his ten rubles. . . . I'll grow up and, I'll challenge him myself, and I'll kill him!" (pp. 206-207)

Ilyusha is mortally ill with tuberculosis and has been outcast by the other boys after stabbing Kolya, who had been his friend and champion. Kolya is another boy with a Fatherson injury: his father died when he was an infant, and his mother did not remarry. Dostoevsky implies that Kolya still turns to his dead father for strength, as in a poignant but comic sequence when he discovers in one of his father's books the names of the "founders of Troy" and stumps his peers and even his teachers by asking them if they know the answer. Alyosha becomes Kolya's friend and mentor, a kind of father in older brother mode, and reconciles him to Ilyusha, toward whom Kolya assumes a brotherly role during the boy's last days as he lies moribund. These pathetic scenes are piercingly beautiful, especially the relationship of the dying boy to his father, who he urges

> "Papa, don't cry. . . and when I die, you get some nice boy, another one . . . call him Ilyusha, and love him instead of me . . . ."
> "And don't ever forget me, papa . . . . visit my grave . . . and one thing more, papa, you must bury me by the big stone where we used to go for our walks, and visit me there with Krasotkin, in the evenings . . . . And I'll be waiting for you . . . . Papa, papa."
> (p. 561)

The beauty of his boy's faith in him ennobles Snegiryov, at least momentarily:

> "Ilyushechka told me, Ilyushechka," he exclaimed at once to Alyosha, "he was lying there one night and I was sitting by him, and he suddenly told me: 'Papa, when they put the dirt on my grave, crumble a crust of bread on it so the sparrows will come, and I'll hear that they've come and be glad that I'm not lying alone.'"
> "That's a very good thing," said Alyosha, "you must do it more often."
> "Every day, every day!" the captain babbled, brightening all over, as it were. (p. 771)

IVAN AND THE DEVIL

Alyosha and Dmitri were initiated in dreams; Ivan's dreamlike story of the Grand Inquisitor also points towards initiation. But Ivan must go through a much darker night and encounter a father more reprobate than his own to reach his Fatherson maturity; in a "brain fever," he encounters the devil himself as "buffoon" (p. 645).

Smerdyakov murdered old Karamazov from uncontrolled hatred: "this desire got such a hold on me it even took my breath away" (p. 628). But the lackey also killed his father and master because he believed in nothing, had felt belittled and unmirrored all his life, and could not idealize. In fact, he had begun a little to look up to Ivan, who alone he felt had treated him as a man, and not as a "fly" (p. 632). The two held long talks on the absurdities of Christianity and agreed that in the absence of ultimate values "all is permitted." Smerdyakov saw, as Ivan did not, that Ivan hated his father and would not be sorry if Dmitri killed him. Smerdyakov interpreted Ivan's actions as a compact between them that he should kill the old man and dealt with his own guilt (Smerdyakov was not entirely a psychopath) by putting the larger share of the blame onto Ivan. The "anything is permitted" philosophy is the grandiose inflation of the unmirrored self freed also from the containing power of the idealized selfobject. Ironically, neither Ivan nor Smerdyakov truly believed it, and Smerdyakov was able to pretend to do so only through an idealizing (or perhaps a twinship) transference toward Ivan.

Ivan finally recognizes that Smerdyakov killed his father, and that he himself bears guilt for the murder. Ivan determines to tell this in court but the night before falls into a delirium and dreams of the devil: he appears as a slightly seedy gentleman, a "sponger" on the good will of his betters, who—like old Karamazov—boasts of his buffoonery. In a powerful argument against lucid dreaming, Ivan struggles to convince himself (and perforce the devil) that the devil is only a figment of his imagination, unreal, and hence of no moral or spiritual importance to him.

> "Not for a single moment do I take you for the real truth," Ivan cried, somehow even furiously. "You are a lie, you are my illness, you are a ghost. Only I don't know how to destroy you, and I see I'll have to suffer through it for a while. You are my hallucination. You are the embodiment of myself, but of just one side of me . . . of my thoughts and feelings, but only the most loathsome and stupid of them. (p. 637)

But the devil is more than Ivan's personal shadow; he is vitally interested in having Ivan accept him as real. He says, "And, after all, who knows whether proof of the devil is also a proof of God?" The devil is a spirit of unbelief who wishes above all to believe, but can do so only if he can convince Ivan—rightly—to believe. His goal is to save his own soul by saving Ivan's soul (p. 645).

> Though I am your hallucination, even so, as in a nightmare, I say original things, such as have never entered your head before, so that I'm not repeating your thoughts at all, and yet I am merely your nightmare and nothing more." (p. 639)

The devil is a true comedian and ironically reveals the connection between the reprobate absurdity of the failed father, who "negates" the Fatherson, and the redeeming comic spirit of *The Brothers Karamazov* as a whole. The devil is a "negative" selfobject (see chapter 4), one who points toward the depth and reality of Ivan's self by negating it and then himself, like the material, feminine *prakriti* in the Indian Sankhya system of philosophy who dances before the spirit, *purusa,* hiding him, yet intending ultimately to show *purusa* to himself by revealing in her dance that she is not (she shows that her being is only the witnessing *purusa* himself). Ivan is, therefore, in a way correct to deny the devil's reality: *"le diable n'existe point."* But this is a wonderful joke: the "nonexistent" devil—whose nonreality is shown in his being a "sponger" on the reality of others—is a halfwitting agent of God, and of the Fatherson archetype, and his nature and function is to lead Ivan to his own Fathersonhood. As the devil himself expresses this perplexing matter:

> By some pre-temporal assignment, which I have never been able to figure out, I am appointed to 'negate,' whereas I am sincerely kind and unable to negate . . . . We understand this comedy: I, for instance, demand simply and directly that I be destroyed. (p. 642)

> I am perhaps the only man in all of nature who loves the truth and sincerely desires good. (p. 647)

The humor in *Karamazov,* half-consciously expressed by the devil, is in the self-negation of the reprobate father, his intrinsic character of dissolving his own ego pretensions and pointing toward the self pole of the axis, revealing himself (mostly unconsciously, in spite of himself) as a selfobject, albeit a negative one, rather than a self. The devil tells Ivan a story that reveals the joy of accepting selfobjecthood, and the absurdity of the ego's self-pretensions.

> There was, they say, a certain thinker and philosopher here on your earth who "rejected all—laws, conscience, faith," and above all the future life. He died and thought he'd go straight into darkness and death, but no—there was the future life before him. He was amazed and indignant: "This,"he said "goes

against my convictions" . . . . he was sentenced to walk in darkness a quadrillion kilometers . . . and once he finished that quadrillion, the doors of paradise would be opened to him . . . .

Well, so this man . . . stood a while . . . and then lay down across the road: "I don't want to go, I refuse to go on principle!" Take the soul of an enlightened Russian atheist and mix it with the soul of the prophet Jonah who sulked in the belly of a whale for three days and three nights—you'll get the character of this thinker lying in the road.

Ivan tries to bait the devil, asking, "Well, so is he still lying there?" The devil replies:

The point is that he isn't. He lay there for nearly a thousand years, and then got up and started walking . . . he arrived long ago . . . .

The moment the doors of paradise were opened and he went in, before he had been there two seconds . . . he exclaimed that for those two seconds it would be worth walking not just a quadrillion kilometers but a quadrillion quadrillion, even raised to the quadrillionth power! In short, he sang "Hosanna". . . . (p. 644)

Ivan gets up the next day and walks the first of his quadrillion miles, to the witness stand where he tells the court that he is guilty of his father's death because he put Smerdyakov up to it; but he is not believed, since he is still locked in his "brain fevered" struggle with himself over God and the Fatherson. But the nobility of his gesture, although not understood by her, will win for him the love of Katerina Ivanovna,[3] and Alyosha, at least, has confidence that his brother will recover from his illness.

THE SUFFERING FATHER

To debase the ego self, freely suffer for the sake of others who suffer (Dmitri's "wee ones"), is ideal Fatherhood for Dostoevsky. This is a Christian vision and offers to Jungian and self psychology a kind of

---

3. All three brothers Karamazov win women's love because they can suffer for others. If a true Russian folk tale must end in a wedding (Propp), *The Brothers Karamazov* ends with three betrothals: Alyosha and Liza, Dmitri and Grushenka, Ivan and Katerina.

selfobject and archetype quite different from the idealized lawgiver (or hated tyrant) usually associated with Father. A true father of the type, like Father Zosima, realizes that "everyone is guilty for everyone else" (p. 298). Buffoonery is a symptom of the narcissistic suffering of the ego self faced with its lack of control over selfobject "others" and incipient sense of its own selfobjecthood toward them. It can thus be a way station on the road to acceptance of one's lowness and guilt and can lead toward a sense of solidarity with others since "all people are 'wee ones' " (p. 591). It is foreign to modern individualism to idealize such a "weak," seemingly passive father image, but Dostoevsky makes this possible for us within the world of his novel. He shows in Father Zosima's history how bold a "suffering" father can be.

Zosima was a wild young officer much like Dmitri, and forced a duel with the young man who married the woman he loved. The night before their encounter, Zosima had a change of heart and, after standing up to his rival's first shot, threw away his pistol and asked the man's pardon. At the same time, he announced his decision to become a monk and his conviction that all are guilty before all, that the world is wholly and intimately interconnected, and that this truth is realized in love. The young Zosima's vision was ridiculous but provocative, and he later reported that his fellow officers and local society "laughed at me, and yet they loved me" (p. 300). Like Alyosha later (and Prince Mishkin in Dostoevsky's *The Idiot*), Zosima became "a sort of holy fool" (p. 301).

Dostoevsky's narrator, the predominant carrier of his voice as a writer in *Karamazov,* is himself a "muddlehead" but a lovable one just because he lacks "author"-ity and never controls the characters he describes. He does not need deconstruction because he never pretends to power. The "unplanned," seemingly spontaneous form of the novel betrays the narrator's faith in *God's* plan in the lives of the Karamazov sons and their father, a plan that the narrator assists by humble means, placing himself at the level of his characters, moving among them, and mirroring their natures and struggles. Richard Pevear says in his introduction to the novel, "the idea stated by the elder Zosima, that 'each of us is guilty before all and for all,' is fully embodied in the fates of the Karamazovs" (p. xiv). It is also personified in the style and perspective of the narrator. The novel is about the posthumous redemption of the reprobate father in his sons, and of the sons by their brothers. The spirit of self- (and other-) contempt in old Karamazov is found also in Ivan and his Inquisitor, in Smerdyakov, in Dmitri, and even in the young Zosima. His naive and sentimental but sympathetic "muddle-headedness" is found in Alyosha, ironically in Ivan's devil, and in the narrator. The novel swings between the poles of Father as evil fool and as holy fool, and its aim is to transform the evil, contemptuous fool into a holy, compassionate one. In the process, the narrative takes the perspective of a son and brother to the Karamazovs, a perspective clearly suggested by the character of Alyosha, with whom the narrator is fascinated.

Although this is never directly stated or even clearly implied, I suggest that the novel is more satisfying and complete if we infer that the narrator is none other than Ivan, writing thirteen years after he has recovered from the "creative illness" in which we leave him at *Karamazov*'s end (Ellenberger, 1970). As the narrator says, the published text is only the first half of a two-part novel (or "biography") of the life of Alyosha Karamazov, and much of it reads like hagiography, such as the "life and teachings" of Father Zosima which forms Book Six. The narrator clearly loves Alyosha and is writing to celebrate and become closer to him. Ivan, the writer in the family, often declares his love for his saintly brother even though he does not understand him and cannot yet be like him. Just as Alyosha was saved by love for his guru Zosima, Ivan—both as character and as narrator—is in the process of being saved by his beloved brother Alyosha; the seven hundred pages of his narrative is another part of the "quadrillion miles" Ivan must walk to reach paradise.

Everyone loved Alyosha, including old Karamazov who had "come to love him sincerely and deeply, more than such a man had, of course, ever managed to love anyone else" (p. 19). Although his evil lives after him, Karamazov has also left behind his love of Alyosha. Ivan's devil/psychopomp is evidently a form of old Karamazov leavened by Alyosha's spirit. The action of the novel transforms not only Ivan's character but that of his father, and in a way each is carried down the long road on the other's back: the narrator/Ivan works old Karamazov's buffoonery toward its potential of loving acceptance, and the old man's mocking recognition of ego nullity conveys the proud Ivan to the same goal.

CHAPTER 6

Fatherson and the King

He who is willing to work gives birth to his own father.

Kierkegaard, Fear and Trembling

A friend recently suggested to me that Robert Bly and his fellow men's seminar leaders (Michael Meade, Robert Moore, and others) form a kind of father-sons clan akin to the old TV series *Bonanza,* with Bly being, of course, the Ben Cartwright of the family. I joked that James Hillman could not reasonably be understood as Bly's "son" and seemed in that context more like an eccentric uncle. But it does seem evident that some sort of ritual initiatory process is at work in the men's movement, and that this centers around images of the sacred king and Father now working their way back into the collective psyche. As Moore (Moore and Gillette 1990) and Bly (1990) put it, their seminars aim to help men get initiated and become mature "men of power." For Bly this implies taking on the adult man's "fierceness," while for Moore it means achieving "man psychology" (which he opposes to "boy psychology"). As a male still struggling with "initiation," I sympathize with their fantasy of the *Man* (that's spelled M-A-N, I recall from the Bo Diddley song), but from Fatherson perspective I question their conclusion that becoming a man means literally giving up the boy, or encompassing his nature within a fantasy of maturation. Consider the irony in Shakespeare's words about the over-mature King Lear: "ripeness is all" (*King Lear* 5.2.10).

Moore and Bly view Father under the sign of the king and their sense of being supported, furthered, inspired, strengthened, and loved by His Majesty is convincing. This upward-looking love felt by the son for his father, by the servant for his master, and by the subject for his king (even the creature for his God) is perhaps the missing ingredient in Dostoevsky, and even more so in Mark Twain. In *Karamazov* when the young Zosima—on his way to the duel— begs forgiveness of his servant Afanasy whom he had struck the day before and kisses his feet, the man "was completely astounded: 'Your honor, my dear master, but how can you ... I'm not worthy ... ,' and he suddenly began weeping himself ... , covered his face with both hands, turned to the window, and began shaking all over with tears" (p. 298). Perhaps these were not (as Zosima thought) tears of thanksgiving at being treated as a human being by his master but an expression of hurt at the loss of the king in his master, whose self-humiliation was felt as an injury to the self of the servant. Ananda Coomaraswamy quotes an Indian as protesting that he is not his master's servant but his *slave,* the point being that the man's slave status both exalts the master and also increases the slave's degree of participation in his master's being.

Robert Moore has developed an ambitious structural theory of the masculine realm, organizing the male psyche into two polarities placed at right angles to one another: the *Warrior* versus the *Lover* on one pole, and the *King* versus the *Magician* on the other.[1] The Magician is a representation of clear-sighted knowledge, specifically of the "observing ego." His psychic objectivity distances the Magician from life and opposes him to the King who is at the center of life, as its principle of order and its creative source. The Magician's negative shadow poles are the manipulator, who stands back and takes a puppet-master's attitude toward others whom he controls, and the innocent victim, who controls passive-aggressively. The Lover expresses such things as enjoyment of beauty, oneness with life, and spiritual union with the world and other humans. His shadow poles are the addicted lover (the Don Juan or sensualist) and the impotent man. Sadism and masochism are the shadow poles of the Warrior, who in his "fullness" represents the aggressive power needed to act decisively in the service of the highest self values.

----

1. There is an apparent correlation between Moore's scheme of the masculine archetypes and George Dumézil's structural theory of the ideology of Indo-European society (Littleton 1966; also see Collins 1993). According to Dumézil, the proto-Indo-European culture understood society—or rather the masculine half of society—to be organized in a tripartite structure of "functions," with the highest function, that of kingship, being divided in two, magical versus juridical. This is clearly very similar to Moore's King versus Magician dimension. Dumézil's second function is the warrior, and the third—the most inclusive—is that of the common people, whose function is fertility. In India the gods representing the third function, the Asvins, are noted as dancers, musicians, and lovers, all roles which fall within Moore's Lover archetype. The obvious question is whether the Dumézil-Moore correspondence is due to the archetypal universality of this pattern or simply to its historical prevalence in Indo-European societies.

In Moore's terms, the Karamazovs mostly act within the Magician and Lover archetypes. The negative Magician—manipulator and "innocent" (for whom Dostoevsky's term is "buffoon")—is embodied in old Karamazov, Smerdyakov, and Ivan. The Lover is epitomized in Alyosha's vision of the oneness and sacredness of all men and the physical cosmos but is also present, negatively, in old Karamazov's and Dmitri's "sensuality." The Warrior is found mostly in Dmitri, who at times is sadistic and much more often a masochist; but the archlover Alyosha is himself referred to at the moment of his initiation as a "fighter" who will stand up for his vision of oneness with all men (p. 362). This is a good example of how the opposite poles (as understood by Moore) of Lover and Warrior can be unified. There is little "king energy" in *Karamazov*. In Dostoevsky's liberal, democratic vision of a truer Russia—as in the America of Toqueville and Twain—there is no strong center, no adequate carrier of the king image, although the figure of Father Zosima and the institution of elders keeps the king at least alive.[2]

Moore's scheme organizes the masculine into a fourfold pattern of archetypes, each of which is understood to contain positive and negative poles as degenerate or limited aspects of itself. As noted above, the Magician archetype has as an active pole the manipulator and as a passive pole the pseudo-naive innocent. Moore's approach is an improvement on the usual perspective which sees each archetype as having a shadow side hiding behind a good side (e.g., the devouring versus the nurturing Mother); he sees that *both* partial perspectives are negative, simply by virtue of being partial. It helps to understand Moore's viewpoint if we reframe it in Kohutian terms. The archetype as a whole can be understood following Kohut as a "self" (or "nuclear self"), while the poles of the archetype are only partial, constituent structures, which turn negative when they are torn from the archetype "in its fullness." Thus the mature Magician has within himself both manipulative and innocent potencies, but these are integrated within his "fullness" and do not result in

---

2. In the larger society there is only a Czar, the tyrant who sentenced Dostoevsky and his comrades to be shot and commuted the sentence (to hard labor in Siberia) only after three of them had been blindfolded and tied to the stake. The peripheral issue of ecclesiastical courts, upon which Ivan wrote a tongue-in-cheek treatise, can be understood in terms of a "church kingship," as can the Grand Inquisitor's fantasy that the church has taken Caesar's place.

abusive, split-off behavior. Manipulation on its own, or willful buffoonery, are "breakdown products" (in Kohut's language); they result when the Magician-self cannot hold its center.

The center of the masculine psyche or self *as a whole*, according to Moore, is the King archetype. Robert Bly's concerns also revolve about the king. Both authors agree that we have far too little king these days, and consequently too little father. I will try to explicate the kingship views of Bly and Moore, alluding to those of Jung, Erich Neumann, John Weir Perry, A. M. Hocart, and Henri Frankfort upon whose thinking they rest, and then compare them with the kingship theory found in Indian culture. Finally, I will try to see what light kingship studies per se can shed on the Fatherson.

In 1976 I finished a Ph.D. dissertation, begun in 1970, on the origins of the Brahman-King relationship in Indian social thought. The origins of this work were in my own king- and father-absence, but also in my relationship at that time with Indian mentor and guru figures (one of whom, the novelist Raja Rao, suggested the topic). I didn't know it then but my research was implicitly a struggle against these "fathers," who seemed to endanger my sense of self even while offering me the security of a bond with strong older males which enhanced my self-sense. As I suggested in the introduction, the fight appeared to me as a battle for ownership of my self; the question was, *Whose* is this self? They seemed to want to own it and to turn me—like Smerdyakov—into their "lackey." I in turn sought to defeat them and show the error in their "non-dualist" Vedantic thinking. I took a typically Indian—and typically unconscious—approach to this and appealed to the Vedas, the Father-texts of Indian civilization, to refute the views of these father figures. Struggling like Ivan Karamazov to rid myself of my need for Father I nevertheless found time for five more gurus (three Zen Buddhists, an Alice Bailey theosophist and a Radhasoami spinoff) while writing my dissertation. In analysis, I repeated the whole pattern again while beginning, this time, to achieve a grain or two of consciousness. My father's bee was still buzzing in my bonnet. Somehow, it has ceased tormenting me and become calmer, and I can look on my fathers past with respect and even love. But my bee still emits enough buzz to stimulate this project.

Kingship is an enormous topic within the fields of history of religions, cultural history, comparative mythology and folklore, and so on, and has been of intense interest to many civilizations for millennia. A dominant thread in the different ways to understand the king is his *centrality* in society, to which is closely related his *cultural creativity*. As John Weir Perry (1966) sees it, following Jung, the archetypal king represents the Self as center and source of order in the world and in the psyche. He is "Lord of the Four Quarters" not just because he controls territory but because he contains in seed form a fourfold cosmic structure which he creatively imposes on the world or inspires a formless world to assume voluntarily.[3] After "creation," he nurtures those of his subjects who follow the paths ordained for them within this structure. Moore therefore rightly says that the King orders and fertilizes the world and "blesses" or "mirrors" the creatures of the world, seeing—like God on the seventh day—that they are (mostly) good. On the plane of the human father and son, Moore beautifully remarks:

> Young men today are starving for blessing from older men, starving for blessing from the King energy. This is why they cannot, as we say "get it together." They shouldn't have to. They need to be blessed. They need to be seen by the king.... (Moore and Gillette 1990, p. 61)

But the King is mostly evident in his shadow forms of tyrant and weakling, which for Moore are the active and passive poles of the negative King—in Kohutian terms, "breakdown" forms of the archetype. The tyrant arises when the ego identifies with the King archetype, and the weakling appears when the ego feels itself completely cut off from the King. Thus the King's shadow (in classical Jungian fashion) is a function of the ego's relation to the archetype. In proper ego-Self relation to the King, the ego is a servant. In Kohutian language, the ego should accept being selfobject to the King's self. Then, as Moore notes, the ego will "love the lord thy God [read, "the King"] with all thy heart . . ." (ibid., p. 73). But this upward-gazing, idealizing love creates a double selfobject structure (as discussed in Chapter 2). In terms of ego and King:

---

3. For an example, in the Indian context, of the world's voluntary submission to the king, see Inden (1990, p. 233).

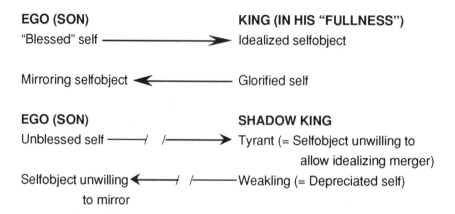

That is, the blessing King is glorified by the same ego whom he blesses; the ego mirrors back the glory of the idealized King. When the ego does not feel blessed and refuses to mirror the King, the latter is robbed of his glory and becomes a weakling/tyrant. This is from the ego's viewpoint. From an archetypal perspective (Hillman or Jung in *Answer to Job*), we could start from the King archetype's failure to "bless." As Moore noted on the human plane, why should we expect the ego to "get it together" and mirror the King when the King tyrannizes him and fails to bless him? Why not take the old bastard down and make him a weakling? Thus arises the fiery demon energy in the ego/son which would waste the King's world and harrow his heaven. On the personal level, Laius's brutality rouses Oedipus's castrating revenge.

IRON JOHN'S QUEST

Robert Bly's recent, justly celebrated book *Iron John* (1990) is about the initiation of boys (of any age) into manhood. Bly landscapes the tale that forms the bedrock of his book with a Persian garden of poetry, stories, and reflections; he aims to reveal through his amplifications of the eponymous story the underlying initiatory structure of an archetypal boy's path to maturation.

Bly's translation of the tale—which is close to that of Padraic Colum (1944)—takes ten pages to tell, and should be read in its entirety. What follows is a summary.

> Near a King's realm was an enormous forest into which men had disappeared, and which it was therefore forbidden to enter. A hunter won the King's permission to go there and discov-

ered a hair-covered, rusty brown colored Wild Man at the bottom of a pond. The Wild Man was placed in an iron cage in the King's courtyard. The King's son lost his golden ball in the cage, and the Wild Man returned it after the boy agreed to open the cage with the key that was kept under his mother's pillow. The Wild Man departed, carrying on his shoulder the boy who had released him, because the boy was afraid of being beaten for letting the captive go.

In the forest, the Wild Man set the boy the task of watching over a golden spring to make sure that nothing fell into it. Over three successive days, however, the boy allowed his injured finger, a hair from his head, and all his hair to fall into the water; each item turned into gold on touching the water. Iron John was angry and sent the boy out into the world; he went to the court of another king and was put to work first in the kitchen, then the garden. The King's daughter caught a glimpse of the golden light reflected from the boy's hair (which he tried to keep hidden by a kerchief) and asked him to bring her some flowers. For three days, she tried to get the boy to uncover his head, and gave him some golden coins. He would not reveal his hair and gave the coins to the gardener's children.

There was a war, and the King's forces were close to defeat. Iron John gave the boy a war-horse, with which he defeated the King's enemies, but without revealing himself. The King's daughter threw out golden apples at a three-days festival the King gave in hopes of attracting the mysterious knight who had won the battle for him. The boy, in armor given by Iron John, caught all three apples but again gave them to the gardener's children to play with. The King found this out from the gardener and had the boy brought to him; the boy now acknowledged that he was the knight from the battle and the catcher of the apples. The King gave him his daughter, and at their wedding Iron John, now a King, appeared, thanked the boy for rescuing him from the enchantment that had put him on the pond's bottom, and made the boy his heir.

It is significant that the boy protagonist in "Iron John" is the son of a king, and that Iron John himself, who is at the story's beginning a wild man trapped (we later learn) through enchantment at the bottom of a lake, is revealed at the end as a king in his own right. "Iron John" is therefore a story of attaining and regaining *kingship*. At the wedding which ends the tale, we read (in Bly's translation):

> While all the guests were sitting at the table for the marriage feast, the music broke off all at once, the great doors swung open, and a baronial King entered, accompanied in procession by many attendants.
>
> He walked up to the young groom and embraced him. The guest said: "I am Iron John, who through an enchantment became turned into a Wild Man. You have freed me from that enchantment. All the treasure that I own will from now on belong to you." (p. 232)

We are reminded of "Beauty and the Beast," where a prince has been changed into bestial form and is returned to his true royal shape through the faithful self-development into adulthood of an adolescent. We suggested the tale was as much the story of Beauty's father as it was of Beauty or the Beast. The old king needed to gain psychological femininity, and to establish a Fatherson relationship with the Beast, his son-in-law and heir. Bly arrives at a similar conclusion regarding the intention of "Iron John":

> As we read this last scene, we say in some shock: "Whose story was this?" We assumed it was the boy's story; but we see it may be the Wild Man's story. (p. 232)

But what does Iron John learn in the story, how does *he* develop? Bly emphasizes the West's rejection of the wild man and sees the story as moving to return him to his rightful dignity. This is the "ego" interpretation again: it is the Western ego's fault that Iron John was consigned to the mud of the lake's bottom, and therefore it is up to the Western ego, in the form of the king's young son, to return him to his kingship in the city, at the heart of culture. Here Moore's diachronic/developmental and Bly's ego-historical theories of the masculine must be supplemented by James Hillman's synchronic archetypal approach, which would suggest that we seek the cause of Iron John's exile in his own nature rather than in the sins of the Western ego or the puerility of the boy who needs to seek him out.

Perhaps Iron John was not just an innocent victim. I note that there are, in fact, three kings in our story: the boy's father, the king whose daughter he wins, and Iron John. The story has similarities to others in which a father loses his son and regains him, now as an adult, after the son achieves a quest. We have seen in some of these stories that the middle-aged father often needs initiation as much as the son. In "Iron John," the second king (the princess's father) has the common fairy-tale problem of letting go of his daughter; this was also true of Beauty's father. The boy's father also has a problem at the beginning of "Iron John." He is king of a land which contains an enormous, deadly forest into which men cannot go because they will be swallowed up by it. This is the initial scene: the civilized king ruling in his castle, holding sway over the fields and villages of his realm, and adjacent to it the wild man, Iron John, ruling over the perilous forest from his place on the lake's floor. Although contiguous, the realms are not in contact. Both kings suffer from one-sidedness.

Between the king and Iron John the story introduces two mediating figures: the intrepid hunter who enters the forest and discovers Iron John, and the king's son who becomes Iron John's protégé and eventually leads him back to civilization in honor. After the hunter finds Iron John, the king locks the wild man in a cage in his castle. This amounts to a preliminary, and abortive, attempt to conquer the wild side and keep it trapped within the civilized. The effort fails because the king's son becomes entranced by the wild man (this is my interpretation of his golden ball falling into Iron John's cage). It fails, furthermore, because the key to the cage is "under the Queen's pillow." Bly reads this fact as pointing to an oedipal conflict, which is plausible, but it might also mean that the queen—the king's and the boy's femininity—is attracted to the wild man and dreams of him as she lies in bed beside her husband. Iron John is released when he gives back the boy's golden ball, but the boy realizes that in letting the wild man go he has been disloyal to his father and fears he will be beaten by him. Both because he is attracted to Iron John and because he is afraid of his father's wrath, the boy goes with Iron John into the forest.

It is clear that the boy undergoes initiation in the forest, and Bly has written beautifully of this ritual. I would look at the entire process, however, as affecting the self of the wild man just as much as it does the maturing psyche of the boy, so that the boy's initiation also redeems the wild man (and by implication the boy's own father and his bride's father). The essence of Iron John's teachings seems to be psychic objectivity or discrimination, specifically the capacity to refuse a premature ownership of the pure "gold" of unconscious wholeness. This wholeness, which is initially symbolized by the boy's golden ball, is also represented by the gold fish in the magical spring which the boy is made to guard, by his own finger and hair turned gold through touching the water of this well, by the gold coins given him by the king's daughter, and finally by the golden apples which the boy as champion receives from the princess.

In all cases the youth must give the gold away or hide it, showing that he is not inflated or possessed by the precious metal. Let us look a little more closely at the boy's first test, beside the spring. He is told by Iron John, "Do you see this golden spring? It is clear as crystal, and full of light. I want you to sit beside it and make sure that nothing falls into it, because if that happens it will wrong the spring. I'll return each evening to see if you've obeyed my order" (Bly 1990, p. 252). As often with three part tests, the boy's performance deteriorates from day to day. He is fascinated by the spring, and on the third day is caught, Narcissus-like, gazing into his own eyes reflected in the pool. His hair falls into the water and is turned to gold. We are evidently near the realm of King Midas, and that king's mistake and the boy's are the same: the loss of distance between ego and Self (in Jungian terms) or between self and archetypal selfobject (in Kohutian terms). But consider now the parallel condition of the wild man at the beginning of the story: he lies at the bottom of a magical lake, which captures everything it touches and encompasses it within itself. There is no psychic objectivity here but rather a condition of union or—in Schwartz-Salant's terms—a *merger* between Iron John and his archetypal context. The situation is quite similar to that of Merlin trapped in his white thorn hedge, as analyzed by Heinrich Zimmer (1971). The magician has been caught in his own snare and is enchanted by his vision of oneness. He teaches the boy, contrary to his own situation, to love and respect the oneness but to resist its bewitchments.

Who has enchanted the wild man? Our story does not say, but Merlin's example strongly suggests that the fault lies at least partly in the one enchanted. The tests which Iron John sets for the boy are, in fact, tasks which he himself has not been able to achieve and needs help in accomplishing. John must not fall back into his lake, and in resisting the pull of the spring the boy helps the wild man resist his own temptation to sink again into the beloved oneness of Nature. The boy partially fails, and Iron John sends him into the civilized world to continue his education in objectivity. Here, the boy's test is not to identify the sexual beloved with the Self or allow himself to be bought with her gold. In the Merlin story, love was the wizard's downfall. Perhaps, then, it was a beautiful witch who enchanted Iron John and left him in the muck. But the boy will not be seduced, and in passing this test proves himself worthy of inheriting the kingship now bequeathed to him by a revitalized Iron John.

OSIRIS/HORUS THE KING

We have a twofold Fatherson kingship in *Iron John* as in *King Lear* and "Beauty and the Beast." Four thousand years old, another story in which this is so is that of the Egyptian gods Osiris and Horus (Frankfort 1948). Although the story of Osiris as a whole is available only in a version retold by Plutarch, at least two thousand years after the myth's first appearance, it seems clear that its central core includes the following.

> Osiris's twin brother, Seth, trapped Osiris by making a beautiful chest which he offered to anyone whom it fit. Osiris fit the box perfectly, and as he lay in it Seth had it closed and sealed and floated out the mouth of the Nile into the Mediterranean. The chest washed up on a beach and became embedded in a tree trunk which the King of Byblos used to support the roof of his palace. Osiris's and Seth's sister, Isis, followed Osiris to Byblos, and the King's sister (ignorant of the goddess's identity) made her nurse to her child. Isis secretly held the child in the fire to burn away its mortal parts, but the mother saw this and shrieked, thus depriving the child of immortality. Isis opened the tree trunk containing Osiris and sailed away with her brother's body in its chest. She then caused the dead Osiris's penis to become erect and with it conceived a son, Horus. Isis left Osiris in his box where he was found by Seth, who dismembered the body into fourteen parts and scattered them. Isis found and reunited all the parts except Osiris's phallus, and she carved a wooden one to take its place. Later, Osiris came to Horus from the other world and trained him to fight Seth; after a great battle Horus defeated his   uncle and bound him. In the fight Horus was injured in the eye but recovered his sight; he cut off Seth's testicles and placed them in the twin scepters signifying his kingship. Isis then released Seth, and Horus tore off her crown in anger.

As Frankfort notes, the Osiris-Horus myth was paradigmatic for Egyptian kings, the old king (the father) being identified with Osiris, and the new king (the son) with Horus. Speaking of an early text (the "Memphite theology") Frankfort says:

... kingship is conceived in its profoundest aspect, on the plane
of the gods, as involving two generations. . . .

Hence the succession of earthly rulers assumed an unchang-
ing mythological form, Horus succeeding Osiris, at each new
succession, forever . . . .

The concluding phrases which show Horus in the embrace
of his father, though the latter is buried and has become earth,
show that death does not destroy the kings. There is a mystic
community between father and son at the moment of succession, a unity and continuity of divine power. (1948, pp. 33–35)

The dead Osiris is a chthonic god buried in the earth and
manifest in the green vegetation which sprouts from his body.[4] In
this he is similar to the Green Man (Zimmer 1971; Anderson and
Hicks 1990) and to the numerous reflexes of the wild man theme
cited by Robert Bly (1990, pp. 238-249). Iron John embraced by the
muddy lake is homologous with Osiris bound and floating in the
ocean, held fast within the trunk of a tree, or drifting with the Nile
floodwaters. Each can only be redeemed by a "son."

There have been many Jungian interpretations of the Osiris
myth, and two of the most notable, by Erich Neumann and James
Hillman, reproduce in their respective loyalties some of the flavor of
the myth itself. Neumann sees the myth as a crucial step in the
transformation of the masculine principle from a "dying god" whose
phallus is the property of the great Mother into an eternally vigorous "living phallus" who "retains his potency even . . . mummified . . ."
(1954, p. 227). He is the masculine spiritual potency which now
teaches and inspires his hero-son rather than, as in the old matriarchy, being killed and supplanted by him. "Thus the enthronement
and rulership of the son rest upon the spiritualization of the father"
(ibid., p. 247). As Neumann sums up his position:

Between the son who regenerates himself as a hero, his divine
parentage, and the rebirth of the dead father in the son there
exists a fundamental relationship which was formulated as "I
and the Father are one." In Egypt this relationship was mytho-
logically prefigured in the process to which we have repeatedly
drawn attention: Horus, as the avenger of his father, becomes

4. Osiris is also identified with the annual, life-giving floodwaters of the
Nile (Frankfort 1948, p. 191).

the supreme temporal ruler, but at the same time his earthly
power is grounded in the spiritual authority exercised by Osiris.
(Ibid., p. 246

Father and son are united in their enmity towards Seth, the representative of the old matriarchy. Now, for the first time, there is a
true king: "the ever-fruitful patriarch who continually fertilizes the
earth and reigns over its progeny" (ibid., p. 248).

Hillman disapproves of Neumann's excessive deference to
Mother, of what he takes to be Neumann's understanding of the
whole psychic realm and particularly the masculine psychic in terms
of the hero's quest to defeat and tame her. Hillman therefore rejects
Neumann's model of masculine development from the state of
Mother's phallic servant through initiation into "higher masculinity" (Neumann 1954, p. 253) and loyalty to a spiritual father. He
also disapproves of Neumann's identification of Osiris/father as the
self and Horus/son as the ego. Hillman would agree, however, that
"I and the Father are one" and in fact titles two different sections of
his unfinished puer-senex work "the union of sames" (1967, p. 334;
1979, p. 121). He discusses the Osiris/Horus myth as "paradigmatic"
of the son's effort "to redeem the father by surpassing him," by "flying higher and further" than the father (Berry 1973, p. 76). But he
also notes that Odysseus's wife Penelope "acted as did the mother of
Horus, encouraging the son's search for the father's redemption"
(Hillman, 1979, p. 120). The difference between Neumann and
Hillman is that Neumann sees unification of the disjointed father
as the hero-son's task, while the anti-heroic Hillman would celebrate
the father's decay and find father/son union in their shared dissocia-
tion. We may infer that Hillman would be on the side of Seth,
Neumann of Horus.

Returning to "Iron John," we can apply the Osiris myth and
its interpretations to suggest that Iron John lying under water exerts a sort of magnetic pull on the civilized court of the king, and it is
that pull which causes the hunter to venture into the wild man's
forest and to uncover him in his muddy bed. But the essential recipi-
ent of the attraction is the king's son (whom we might call Iron
John's "godson"); the hunter's job is merely to bring Iron John near
enough for the boy to enter his force field. Iron John, the king in
exile in the archetypal wild, seeks vicarious redemption by teaching
the boy not to lose himself—as Iron John himself has done—in the
golden wholeness of the spring/lake; but he draws him precisely

through the attractive power of that world. Huck Finn's pap, another wild man, is lost in a "lazy and jolly" life drinking whiskey in the woods by the big river; Huck himself, although he has a good measure of psychic objectivity toward pap and his life, is also tempted to let himself go in(to) pap's world. Pap is not conscious of needing Huck to redeem him and in fact seeks to pull Huck down to his level. Because pap cannot recognize that he lives in the muck like a pig, he cannot bless Huck; nevertheless, through his negative example Huck does learn to hold himself back somewhat from the temptation to immerse himself for life in the woods away from "sivilization."

Osiris also succumbed to a temptation when he lay down in Seth's beautiful chest. The chest is, of course, the sarcophagus, so we may suggest that the temptation is death in the arms of the Great Mother, represented in our story by Isis. This interpretation is strengthened by the characteristic identification of Isis as the throne of the king, another maternal embrace (Frankfort 1948, p. 43). A blissful but unconscious state of Osiris results, shades of pap Finn on his big river. Like a corpse in the flooded Mississippi, Osiris drifts submerged, "drowned" in the Nile and its fertile mud; the plants grow up out of his body (Frankfort 1948, pp. 30, 191-192). The psychic objectivity (a standpoint outside the flow of the waters) which Osiris lacked becomes manifest in his son Horus, who redeems his father. Horus is a falcon and, as Hillman notes, soars above the father; but the eye of this falcon is the sun. It is said of Horus, "When thou openest thy eye so as to see, it becomes light for everyone"; he is "a falcon radiating light from his eyes" (Frankfort 1948, p. 37). The singleness and consciousness of Horus's eye, the sun, pulls together and centers the drifting, dissociated Osiris, who now becomes through his son's efforts the repository of the night sun, the sun as it sinks beneath the western horizon. Father and son together express now the total solar fact: day and night, system and chaos unified in a single, overarching order.

THE INDIAN KING

Fatherson issues are at the heart of Indian kingship, and the Indian understanding of the king and his relationship to the people and institutions of his realm will be of help in understanding the Fatherson. As Ronald Inden (1990) has demonstrated, the Indian king is before all a world-ordering agent. Indeed, *agency*—the human capacity to remake the world in terms of one's needs, desires, and visions—would seem to be at the heart of much kingship theory, including Robert Moore's understanding of the king as principle of order and creative stimulus. The ideal Indian king is described as "tirelessly active" in the service of *dharma* (a generic term for the the cosmic, social, political, and individual "laws" which should govern the life of each person). The king's own law is to organize, stimulate, and further the laws of the various persons and social groups or classes (called *varnas*) which make up the human world.

> Again and again, hundreds of times, the *dharmas* of all are seen to be set in motion by the king's *dharma*. Because in age after age the primordial *dharmas* are reactivated by the king, his *dharma* is said to be the highest in the world. (*Mahabharata* 12.64.25)

The human king is often identified with the kingly cosmic males who created, or more accurately "emitted" or "stretched out," the world, Prajapati and Purusa. He is, for example, called the *pratyaksa purusa,* "primordial Man visible to the eyes" (Collins 1976) and *mahapurusa,* "great Man" (Inden 1990, p. 229). Like the cosmic man, the king was thought to "stretch" or "roll" out the four quarters of the earth according to his own inner design and to fill them with his progeny (Gonda 1966a). From this perspective, the king is the only complete person, or self, in society and other people ("persons" from our viewpoint, and most of the time from their own) are constituents of his being. Because their selfhood is part of his, they are his to use as he will.

An implication of this understanding of the king was recorded in the 10th century by the Arab traveler Abu Zayd Hasan:

> Among the kings of India, there are some who, when they accede to the throne, have some rice cooked, and served to them in plantain leaves. The king has three or four hundred companions close to him who are willing and without having been forced by him attached to his person. After he has partaken of the rice, he presents some of it to his companions. Each of them approaches in his turn, and takes a small portion which he eats. All those who have eaten of this rice are obligated, when the king dies, or is killed, to be burned to the last man, on the

same day that the king has died. It is a duty which does not
permit delay, and there must remain neither the body nor any
other trace of them. (Quoted in Inden 1990, pp. 215-216)

The same idea is present in the custom of suttee or "widow burning." In both cases, when the "self" dies, all its "selfobjects" must die
with it.

As Inden notes, however, this idea should not be taken too
far, or one-sidedly, and he proposes that Indian society be seen not
as a single form (that of the cosmic man/king) but rather as a "scale
of [related] forms," where higher level entities encompass but do not
dissolve the lower level forms which they include. Thus, in ideal
society, a world king (a *chakravartin*) would rule over a circle
(*mandala*) of subsidiary kings, who in turn would hold sway over
village, caste, and guild chiefs, etc. Agency, which can equally be
called selfhood, thus exists at different levels. The Sanskrit word
kula expresses this fact well; the word literally means "family" or
"group," but in philosophical thought (Kashmiri Shaivism) it has
come to signify any organized agent entity at any level from Siva to
a tuft of grass, something very close in meaning to the expression
"sentient being" in Buddhism. At each level (world, region, district,
caste, family, human being, plant) there is only *one whole self* which
integrates a manifold of parts, although from the perspective of a
lower level the "parts" of the previous self can be seen as selves
possessing their own intrinsic wholeness (see Collins 1991b, 1991c).

For example, in a primary usage the word *kula* designates
the Indian extended family consisting of a married couple, their
unmarried daughters, and their sons and sons' wives and children.
The word sometimes also refers to a longer lineage centering on a
"seed" male ancestor and including his male descendants whether
or not they live in the same household. Such a family is centered on
and headed by a man called a *Karta* or "Maker." Others in the family must stand ready to serve and obey him (Inden and Nicholas
1977, p. 30). His desires, intentions, and qualities are the organizing principle of the *kula* and define its nature or *dharma*. But from
the perspective of one of the *Karta's* sons, while as son he is only a
part of his father's self and *kula*, as husband of his wife and father of
children he is a whole self whose being his dependents complete. As
Inden says, from a political point of view, "The same man was now a
ruler and now among the ruled" (1990, p. 224).

The role of the *Karta* or king, viewed positively, was not to stifle the selfhoods of the members of his family; rather, by being the person he is, the king was able to further the personhoods (*dharmas*) of others. Similarly, in Vaisnava belief, according to the eleventh century thinker Ramanuja, God is ultimately the "inner controller" of men, although at the level of the person each man is a center of initiative, an agent in his own right. The two aspects (called the "centripetal" and "centrifugal" tendencies by Lipner (1986)) balance one another and are united in the idea of *bhakti,* or loving participation by agents of a lower level in the being of a superior. But, as is suggested by use of the same word *kula* for selves at different levels of being, the "selfness" or sense of agency at all levels is identical. This allows us to specify Moore's reified concept of "King energy": what is in question is kinghood (i.e., a quality), and it is found at every level of existence. On the other hand, kinghood exists at lower levels through participation in higher ones. In self psychological terms, "archetypal" kinghood refers to the idealization of and partial merger of a lower level being into the self of a higher one. The king archetype requires two "persons," whom we may call father and son.

Inden describes the Hindu cosmos as seen from this point of view:

> The overlord of the cosmos, Vishnu or Siva, had created the world out of his divine body. The extent of the cosmos in time and space was, accordingly, considered to be a lifetime of the overlord of the cosmos. The smaller periods of time and correspondingly smaller areas of the cosmos were in turn considered the lives of lesser lords. The whole universe was, in other words, thought of as successions, as in a *genealogy,* of the lives of higher and lower lords and their domains. (Inden 1990, p. 235, my emphasis)

Kingship is an emanational, Fatherson affair. What about the other side of the Fatherson as we have described it, the Father's need for salvation by his Son? This is characteristically not explicit in kingship texts, which exalt the morning and noon of kings, but is implied by the fact of royal succession and, ironically, in accounts of the conquest of a failed pretender to universal kingship by a rival king. It is also explicitly treated (although not especially with respect to kingship) in the *sraddha* or funeral texts.

Indian kingship was "(re-)constituted," according to Inden, by the king's royal "progresses" (*yatras*) through the quarters of his realm and by holding court, when tributary agents in the king's realm would come and renew their loyalty to him. Both events occurred yearly during seasons auspicious for them and more definitively at the crucial moments of a new king's accession to the throne and of territorial expansion (war). The classical (and even the earlier Vedic) understanding of kingship similarly speaks of *digvijaya* or "conquest of the quarters" as an essential act to be undertaken by the king, and the ancient "horse sacrifice" (*asvamedha*) also seems to signify the king conquering territory and making it his own by allowing a stallion, his alter ego, to roam freely for a year through unpopulated country and the territory of other kings. This conquest of the quarters was not understood to be a permanent matter. The cosmos was thought to be inherently entropic, tending to "run down" and decay over time into a state of disorder and absence of kinghood. Significantly, it was felt that we are at present in the most entropic of times (*kaliyuga*) and consequently in maximal need of a king (or kingly avatar of a god) to reinstate *dharma*.

Each new king, in most instances the son of the previous king, attempted to "reinstate *dharma,*" the implication being that, to some extent, his father had allowed *dharma* to decline. Among other ways in which the king's renewal of time and space was signified was the construction of a temple. In cases where the temple had been begun by the king's father or more remote ancestor,

> successive rulers made their distinctive additions to the temple complex . . . . They treated it as a scale of forms. That is, each succeeding emperor saw the temple . . . as modified by his polity, as a new whole, a more complete, truer version of the divine presence than those of his predecessors, which, encompassed in his own work, had become parts of that work. (Inden 1990, p. 256)

The son puts together the more or less fallen-apart father, and in completing him achieves the father's unaccomplished purposes. In a Vedic text, the fire god Agni is said to put together again his father Prajapati, after the latter had fallen apart in the act of emitting the cosmos. Because of this deed, the father, Prajapati, is "called by the name of the son," Agni (see Collins and Desai 1986). Thus the son makes the father immortal in the act of superseding him.

A king who failed in his efforts to reorder the world dharmically, with himself in its center, was thought to have lost his "de-
termination" (*yatna*) or the grace of the god who originally infused
him with the tireless energy (*tejas*) inherent in a king. He had to be
replaced by a new king, who would reorder the realm allowed by the
old king to fall into disorder. Here, again, it was not a matter of
simply overthrowing the old and bringing in the new, but of sub-
suming the old under the new order and so actualizing what the old
king had intended but failed to carry out. Inden describes in this
context the replacement of the Chalukya empire in central India by
the Rashtrakutas, who then used the design of the Chalukya flag as
a subsidiary element in their own flag.

Indian stories and myths abound with examples of this
theme of renewing kingship by defeating and relativizing an old
king. Good examples are the overthrow of the evil King Kamsa by
Lord Krishna (his nephew) and of King Bali by the dwarf avatar of
Vishnu. In such stories we often find that the old king, formerly
characterized as a demon, becomes a devotee of the new king and is
relativized as a "participant" (*bhakta*) in his kingdom. In the story of
Bali, the demon king who pretends to lordship of the cosmos grants
Vishnu's dwarf avatar a seemingly modest gift of "three paces of
land for a fire altar" (Dimmitt and van Buitenen 1978, p. 80-82).
The dwarf then expands to the god's universe-filling dimensions,
and with his three paces strides across the "three worlds" that com-
prise the cosmos. There is no place left for his foot at the end of the
final step, so he puts it on the head of the demon. In many sculp-
tural images of this scene, we see Bali under Vishnu's foot, looking
up at the god with eyes of rapt adoration. After thus "stretching out"
the world anew, reimposing on it the law of his own dharmic kingship, Vishnu gives to Bali the kingship of the netherworld: the old
king, who was not fit to be a Chakravartin, is redeemed as a mem-
ber of Vishnu's *mandala* of tributary kings. He becomes capable of
expressing kinghood in his own, underworldly, realm because he
participates with love (*bhakti*) in the universal kinghood of the god.
In Kohutian terms, Bali achieves agent selfhood through the idealized selfobject, Vishnu, toward whom the demon accepts the role of
mirroring, glorifying selfobject. In this way, the demon and other

"failed" kings lose their fatherhood and become like sons of their conquerors, from whom eventually they receive a renewed (but relative, lower level) Fatherhood.[5]

Demonic kingship raises and begins to answer a question for our overall analysis of the Fatherson, that of its relation to the feminine. In the discussion of *King Lear* I argued that the old father/king needs "psychological femininity"; in treating the Osiris myth and "Iron John," I claimed that their protagonists may be too much in thrall to the feminine, i.e., to a primitive vision of psychological wholeness. The demon king is simultaneously too rigid and too chaotic; he embodies a principle of order that is really disorder, an order out of keeping with *dharma*. The demon's order implies a refusal to be for the sake of others and so to be ("only") part of a larger order; it is an effort to organize the world around one's own wishes without oneself accepting the passive, mirroring selfobject role toward another. Self-centered, egotistic order of this sort is particularly suspect in mid-life and later, when the ego needs to let go and allow itself to be superseded by its "son." The problem with the mature masculine, Robert Moore's cynosure, is that in mid-life it may tend to become demonic and refuse to let itself dissolve.

Ironically, an overly rigid, demonic king or Father is already caught in the chaotic waters, although he does not know it. Refusal to acknowledge reliance on the feminine source brings about vulnerability to the unconscious—and negative— feminine. The Indian king, like the kingly gods of whose nature he partakes, arises in and from the precosmic waters. Vishnu is often represented sleeping on the waters between moments of cosmic manifestation, and the true king remembers as he rules that his ordering energy and capacity to fertilize rest on a deep ocean of potentialities from which he can draw. In India, this deep ocean is called *brahman* and is socially represented by the Brahman class or *varna*. The king, according to Indian theory, is born from the *brahman* and must not lose contact with it. To assure this, he must have a Brahman advisor, called a *purohita,* who embodies the king's origins (Collins 1976). A demonic king is one who has forgotten *brahman* and thinks he is his own source. But this forgetting of *brahman* does not mean that *brahman*

---

5. Robert Goldman (1978) has discussed at length several kinds of quasi-father/son relationships in Indian culture. Although his approach is classical Freudian, it is very useful to realize that guru-disciple, god-devotee and king-vassal relationships have a father-son structure.

does not exist for the demon king; it simply means that *brahman* is manifested in negative form, for example, as the bloodthirsty Indian "goddesses of the tooth," Western parallels to whom are found in King Lear's "serpent toothed" daughters. In the mythology of the great Goddess, a buffalo demon, who seeks to set himself up as the ruler of the universe, is torn apart by the martial feminine astride a tiger.

The father/king must support, further, and bless his son or tributary and, through his dharmic ordering of the world, help him to overcome the chaos which is often represented as a negative female. Conversely, the old king himself must be saved from chaos by his son or by another king more fitted than he at this world-historic moment to extend his creative ordering out across the entropic world. But the disorderly waters are also a nurturing source and, as we discovered earlier, are a feminine support and *tertium* for Father and Son. There is a "beingness" prior to the king's order from which that order grows and which stimulates it to spread creatively across the worlds. Although it seems natural, from a senex or patriarchal viewpoint, to image this "beingness" as feminine, a bisexual interpretation of the world is often understood in Indian thought as inappropriate for the original (or preoriginal) state of things, which is conceived (for example, in the Rig Vedic "Hymn of Creation") as prior to sexual differentiation (Collins 1975). *Brahman* "in its fullness" is also prior to the masculine/feminine split, although it is in many contexts implicitly or explicitly feminine.

AGNI AND VARUNA

The Indian king has his source in the waters, and his installation involves bathing and the pouring of water and other liquids on his body (*abhisheka*). As Inden notes, "the ceremonial bath was a rite that . . . imbued the king with the divine power or energy" of Vishnu or Siva (1990, p. 236). Already in the Vedic period (pre-1000 B.C.E.), the kingly gods originate in the precosmic waters and perform their actions of ordering and fertilizing the cosmos in and from the waters. The arch-father and kingly god Varuna was mentioned in discussing the Sunahsepa story (introduction); while he is sometimes, as in that story, a tyrant king who would have a man cut off his son's life before the boy can grow to manhood, Varuna is also the god most closely associated with the waters. The primordial waters are seen from two perspectives in the Vedas. Most often they appear precosmically as imprisoned in the belly of a demon/serpent, Vrtra (whose name was evocatively translated as "Holdfast" by Ananda Coomaraswamy). The serpent is cut open and slain at dawn by the warrior or hero god Indra, freeing the waters to flow down, opening a mid-space and fertilizing the earth. From this perspective, Varuna is sometimes identified with Vrtra, and is a negative senex or old king needing to be overcome. But most of the time King Varuna dwells in the waters and protects the cosmic order (*rta,* the Vedic term for *dharma*) which inheres in them. At the moment of cosmogenesis, Varuna pours out his "ordinances" like streams of water which flow from heaven to earth and constitute the three worlds as they pass; metaphorically, Varuna's *rta* gushes out like water from a split skin bag or overturned pot. There is consciousness in this "good senex" role, and the *rta*-protecting Varuna is often associated with Agni, the god of fire and inspiration, whose origin is in the waters, and whose presence seems to activate them. Agni is, at times, Varuna's son.

Agni is a puer who is constantly being reborn from his womb in the waters, which are simultaneously his mothers and his wives. Agni is bull and also calf; the waters are cows. Agni inflames them, mates with them, is born from them as his own son, and then retreats back again into their matrix. This daily recurrent process, which is correlated with the rising and setting of the sun as well as with the sacrificial calendar, represents the birth of the cosmos and its "stretching out" into proper shape, but also its periodic falling back into precosmic latency. Both Agni and Varuna are poets and inspirers of poetry among humans. Poetry celebrates and participates in the opening and ordering of the cosmos; like Agni, the poet returns periodically to his origins for renewed inspiration. The poetic function is therefore kingly and creative, and poets are spoken of as "bulls" who emit their verses like seed. Agni fertilizes the waters as their bull and then as calf suckles at their udder; Father Varuna transforms the waters into male seed which he sprinkles on the earth as rain. As the male energic principle in the feminine waters, son Agni is capable of engendering himself and at times dispenses with Mother altogether. He emerges from the Father's belly, is the Father's embryo, and at birth finds the Father's udder. In this drama of masculine parthenogenesis, Agni's mothers come later: after being generated by the Father, Agni sucks the breasts of the Father's daughters or is given heaven and earth as his mothers.

While the Vedic poets generally see water and other liquids as feminine and precosmically as a matrix, they frequently puzzle over this energetic, "Agnic" quality which certain liquids possess: the nourishing power of milk and the invigorating virtue of *soma,* for example, are compared with the fertilizing power of semen and rain. The principle of vigor in milk, which is the cause of its whiteness, is precisely Agni in the waters or in the plants to which the waters descend after the cosmos has been opened. Agni is the latent fire in clarified butter or oil and turns the precosmic waters into the rainfall with which Varuna and other father gods inseminate the earth. As the indwelling spark of life in the Father's seed, Agni is called his "father's father." As a spermatic principle equiprimordial with the waters, Agni is imagined to shine "without fuel" in their depths. He is a kind of tincture or pure culture of maleness and forms the basis in late Vedic religion for a Fatherson cult which has little place for the feminine.

Fatherson unity and renewal without feminine intervention is striking in the *Agnicayana* rite, the construction of the fire altar. Like all late Vedic sacrificial religion, this ceremony imagines a cosmic man, here called Prajapati ("Progenitor"), who is simultaneously identified with the cosmos and with the inner soul or self (*purusa*) in men. An extremely elaborate brick fire altar is constructed over a year's time; it represents the body of the cosmic man and also the world which was extended according to his shape. At the base of this altar is a small anthropomorphic image of gold representing the *purusa* which will regenerate the cosmic man during the rite. This golden man is Agni in his form of "golden embryo" (*Hiranya-garbha*); he is the seed which will grow into a new man and a new cosmos (which is the same thing). The large brick altar and the golden figure, like Agni Hiranyagarbha and the cosmic man, are simultaneously father and son of one another

> Father Prajapati is also the son: because he created Agni, he is Agni's father; and because Agni restored him, Agni is Prajapati's father. (*Satapatha Brahmana* 6.1.2.26; cf Eggeling 1900, 3.153-154)

Seeing Agni and Varuna (or Prajapati) as a single Fatherson being, one is struck by how unheroic and unmatriarchal he is. Both Agni and Varuna are closely associated with the waters but there is no sense that they are attempting to escape a too-tight maternal embrace, or that their masculine potency is limited to being the phallic organ of the Great Mother. One could almost imagine them dispensing with the waters altogether and living a monkish existence in the Rajputana ("King's son") desert! I concluded earlier, however, that the Fatherson needs the anima, just as she does him (Chapter 4). Agni clearly enjoys his sport with the waters, being bull to their cows, and even old Varuna is at times their "husband." Perhaps we could say that in order to live the Fatherson "in its fullness," Agni and Varuna need the waters, that is, in order for each god to surrender his one-sided perspective he needs anima, even though there is pressure in late Vedic religion to minimize this requirement. Varuna would be only the Holdfast serpent without the gift of seeing through its skin to the possibilities of pouring *rta* into a cosmos. Agni might not be willing to join the Father's cosmos in his role as sacrificial priest if he did not have the sweet waters to lay his head on periodically. But Agni and Varuna are primarily oriented toward each other as Fatherson and Sonfather, and in this *coniunctio* achieve a perspective on the waters that frees each of them from the danger of stagnation in their depths.

THE FATHER'S DEATH

It is not surprising that the death of a man's father stimulates intense activity in the Fatherson archetype. In India there is an elaborate series of rituals (the *sraddhas*) lasting years which serve to work out relations between dead father and son and to assure each a place in the larger Fatherson.

At the time of the father's death, the son is instructed to lie on top of the father, and one by one the father's vital essences are transferred into the son's being. Thus the father's self enters into the son, who is given his independent selfhood in this act, but simultaneously saves the father from any bad actions he may have done during his life (*Brhadaranyaka Upanishad* 1.5.17).

One of the most important moments occurs a year after his cremation when the dead father is joined to the group of "near" ancestors or *Pitrs* ("Fathers") (Knipe 1977). We noted above that the son of a dead king tends to subsume his father's world-ordering achievements, such as temple building, under a more encompassing order of his own. But we also noted that the king, like all sons, was given his realm, or initiated into it by his father or an other Father representative such as the god Vishnu. This is the usual Fatherson conflict and as always implies a Fatherson *coniunctio*.

In the *Pitr*-joining rite (*sapindikarana*), the son mixes a ball of rice representing his dead father with other balls representing grandfather and the two previous father generations and reaffirms a lineage of Fatherson solidarity extending back at least seven generations. Knipe (1977) notes that the process is exactly parallel to the reintegration of the cosmic man Purusa or Prajapati when he has fallen apart in the process of cosmogenesis. The sacrificer thus parallels Agni restoring, rearranging, reextending, and renewing Prajapati and is, therefore, like him, in a sense his "father's father." But the circular character of this process is also clear in the *sapindikarana:* the future generativity of the son is dependent on his carrying out the ritual, and the *pindas* are like seeds which produce a son for the son performing the rite.

CONCLUSIONS

The king is the self as center, but centering is only one way in which the self appears. Equally important are the compensatory aspects of anima and Son, forces of dissolution and radical renewal of the old king. It is clear, especially in the Egyptian and Indian data, that the king archetype grows from an origin in watery "chaos." Even when the king has mastered the four quarters and caused the *mandala* of surrounding kings to pay tribute, he cannot escape the circle: he will run down again, become Kamsa, and need a baby Krishna to destroy his decay and re-manifest the eternal Father *dharma* which he has lost. Too great an emphasis on the mature masculine as the all-encompassing final stage of development leads to senex ossification and its unconscious compensation, the feminine flood.

Perhaps the essence of my disagreement with Bly, Moore, and others is their reading of our contemporary king problem as wholly due to ego failure. I have tried to show that the king has a complex nature and that the archetype itself does not assert a final perfection. In terms of Moore's scheme, I would deny that the existence of a "breakdown" or "shadow" king is entirely the ego's fault. The tyrant and the weakling, the King's shadow structure, are in part the result of the ego failing to step aside and allow the king archetype to be incarnated in another. But I would claim that the archetypal king himself intrinsically contains the possibilities of tyranny and weakness.

From a self psychological viewpoint, the question is whether the king needs—in fact, *demands*—selfobject support from others. Moore says

> The Tyrant King manifests . . . most notably in the so-called narcissistic personality disorder. These people really feel that they are the center of the universe . . . and that others exist to serve them. Instead of mirroring others, they insatiably seek mirroring from them. Instead of seeing others, they seek to be seen by them. (1990, p. 67)

But this is implies a fantasy of the mature masculine as completeness, as an absolute endpoint of development. I argue the contrary: the father/king does not exist alone but always and only in a self-selfobject nexus. And this self-selfobject relationship is always two-way: the king *both* mirrors others and is mirrored by them. When the creator or emitter of the cosmos lets beings flow from his body, he is in danger of falling apart. This is why he seeks a mirroring response from those beings; it is their mirroring back of his creative flow that reintegrates him. This is how the Son aids the Father. Likewise, when the Indian king "stretches out" the dharmic world, he is in danger of falling apart unless by activating their dharmas his subjects mirror him back to himself. The king's warrior power (*danda,* literally, his "club") exists primarily to compel his subjects to mirror him. The existence of *danda* does not, however, make the king a tyrant. Only when the *danda* becomes separated from the larger king structure, and the king identifies his nature solely with the *danda,* does he become tyrannical. The king "in his fullness" is not a lone king; to be "full," as Indian thought fully realizes, he must have a Son who, paradoxically, also makes him empty.

The king is a mirroring selfobject to his people, as Moore says, but also an idealizing one: because they look up to him, he too is mirrored and shines in the light of their eyes. In part, the king compels this; in part, it is the people's free act. In compelling a mirroring response, the king exercises power: he is to some degree a controlling tyrant; waiting powerless for the people's love he can seem, or be, a weakling.

CHAPTER 7

De/Centering and
Cultural Cannibalism

*. . . a reproduction of the same that defies
death, in the procreation of the son, this same
of the procreating father.*

Luce Irigaray 1985, p. 27

"While the King's away, the rats will play." This unkind thought occurred to me while reading a *New York Times* piece on a recent Modern Language Association (MLA) convention. I was struck by how rampantly the academic *puer* inflates when the royal center fades. For "royal center" read "Western ego/tradition," "patriarchy," "Christianity," "the Great Books," "Aristotle," or "Allen Bloom": it's not an altogether beautiful image, and I still recall "the meaning of the poem, properly understood" being pronounced by Professor Senex at the University of Chicago, circa 1961. But I didn't find the MLA picture any prettier: the convention hotels seemed packed with desperately irreverent careerists cutting up the canon, playing "Mack the Knife" with "My Father's World." Surely Robert Bly is correct that the "water table" of the father is too low, and that the "'father water'. . . has sunk below the reach of most wells" (Bly 1990, p. 92).

Why, then, is Father *still* the target of assaults from feminism, deconstruction, Lacanian psychoanalysis, and other defenders of "political correctness"? What does this apparent triumph of a decentered orthodoxy signify for the Fatherson? Perhaps in killing, taking apart, and eating the old Father, we are unconsciously erecting a new king in drag to take his place, an armless, phallusless, and centerless Dad, his form that of a doughnut. Do we mourn the archetypal Father even as our disappointment in him tells us to savage his remains? But perhaps he is taking matters into his own hands, raising the psychic pressure or steepening the internal gradient. Perhaps the Father's pit or grave may become an artesian well, and Osiris may erupt again from the waters of the Nile.

Our culture is now living on its psychic capital, endlessly recycling the classics and reducing their insights to the common denominator of mass taste. The packaging of the archetypes in popular culture has progressed very far, and like others the Father has been commodified; nevertheless, I am beginning to think that there may be something in the Fatherson specifically that speaks against this strip-mining of the psyche and could even reverse it. Although the horrors of Disneyland, video games, and politics are hard to face, it is in such places that the king has found his Avalon, and if he rises again it will have to be from media landfills.

A "return of the king" (Arthur in this case) to contemporary Britain is the theme of C. S. Lewis's fantasy novel *That Hideous Strength*. Lewis effectively contrasts the vapid and debased vision of kingship in our media culture with the vigorously real thing: a hairy and rough-spoken Arthur takes on a bureaucratic think tank researching the *in vitro* maintenance of old men's brains—the aim being to preserve the rule of "dead white men" by putting off their deaths indefinitely. Similar territory can be found in the wasteland of political and academic scandal. In the following, we will find that the contrast between true and inauthentic fatherhood is clear in principle but quickly becomes muddled in the daily practice of self-interest common to earthlings, politicians, and literature professors.

THE KING'S DEMON IN TEXAS
ROBERT CARO'S LYNDON JOHNSON

Are the late-cultural cliches of Fatherhood biodegradable? How to digest the redundant masses of plastic Dad that choke our tubes and our heads in an election year? Seeking a conqueror worm to dissolve the tight chains of hydrogen and carbon, I sometimes find myself looking favorably on the MLA's merry band of deconstructionists. The disloyal yet hopeful thought tickles, "did the King do this to us after all?" Who else could be behind media fathers like Ronald Reagan, whose very name seems to smudge my page like a grease stain? Is Father sending up grotesque parodies of himself in place of the genuine article? Perhaps because we cannot idealize Dad any more in real life, but are willing to suspend disbelief on the screen, we were rewarded with a screen president? Yet there is profound violence done to the Fatherson when a vacant man like Reagan, or a weak man like George Bush, or a psychopathic man like Lyndon Johnson incarnates the King for us. In Robert Moore's terms these are not kings at all but manipulator magicians, which I would prefer to call charlatans or impostors, pulling the strings of a King puppet in their own faces and actions. Robert Caro's biography of Lyndon Johnson (Caro 1990) dissects what appears to have been one turning point from real king to impostor. Caro's efforts to deconstruct "Lyndon" (as we called him in Austin) work by contrasting the wily, soulless Johnson with a Man (M-A-N) who had for years carried the King image in Texas, Coke Stevenson, a former Texas governor and Johnson's U.S. Senate opponent in 1948. Let us look at Coke and Lyndon from the vantage points of the Fatherson and of Indian kingship.

Caro writes with sharp nostalgia and unashamed admiration as he describes Stevenson's life on his Texas hill country ranch, and the heart of any Texan would feel pride on reading of the endless work Stevenson put into his beloved land beside the South Llano River, as he cut cedar fence posts, built stone houses and outbuildings with his own hands, and organized the "four quarters" of his fifteen-thousand-acre kingdom. The image I recall most clearly is of an old Coke Stevenson standing at sunset beside the limestone stream that ran by his ranch house, surveying his work and finding it good, if perpetually incomplete. Coke believed that as the ranch, so Texas. His values of hard work and self-reliance translated into conservative and paternalistic politics which expected the same effort from others but which would help the "deserving" among them to reach their potentials. Caro notes that as governor Stevenson had tripled the old-age pensions in the state, increased public welfare payments, reformed the prisons, and brought more humane treatment for the inmates in state mental hospitals. Coke Stevenson was, Caro tries to show, the most beloved politician of his time in Texas and perhaps the most loved since Sam Houston. He incarnated the King without fakery or media hype. Enter Lyndon.

Caro spends much time on Lyndon Johnson's father problem, which he traces to the financial fall and humiliation of Sam Ealy Johnson when Lyndon was thirteen. The elder Johnson, like *his* father, had been a Texas state legislator for twelve years and was a man quite similar to Coke Stevenson in personal integrity and idealism. Lyndon spent as much time as he could with his father and adored and idealized him. He looked like his father and adopted his mannerisms, values, and sense of being special. Sam Johnson fell into debt after a grandiose bid to "make the whole Pedernales Valley Johnson country again" by buying back the family ranch for far too much money (Caro 1990, p. 7). The admiration and respect of the citizens of the hill country turned to ridicule when Sam Johnson became a debtor to everyone in town. "The Johnsons became, in fact, the laughingstock of the town." The formerly proud, "strutting" Sam Johnson fell very far.

> Penniless, doomed to remain in debt until he died, unable to pay his bills in the stores he had to walk past every day, allowed to live in his house only because his brothers guaranteed the mortgage payments, he went to work on a road-grading crew that was building the highway for which he had fought as a legislator, forced to wear work clothes [rather than his customary suit] at last. (Ibid.)

The mirroring response of the people who had formerly idealized Sam Johnson had turned to sadistic "small town sneers and cruelty," and so did Lyndon's attitude toward his father. His older brother, Sam Houston Johnson (himself a court-house character during my years in Austin), said, "It was most important to Lyndon not to be like Daddy." Rather than be seen as a failed idealist like his father, Lyndon "wanted the world to see him . . . as shrewd, wily, sly" (ibid., pp. 5, 7). In Indian terms, Lyndon had in effect decided to become a demon, viewing himself and his own advancement as life's only value and the ideals held by his father and Coke Stevenson as absurd and meaningless. As a politician he would compel, or induce by advertising, the mirroring response he could not allow himself to believe his constituents would give him out of respect or love.

Lyndon hated his personal father and demonstrated throughout his career a hatred and contempt for the archetypal Fatherson. He acted the role of a "professional son" to older men of influence and power, manipulating them to advance himself, while boasting to peers of his success (Caro, 1990, p. 8). He was a good flatterer of the powerful, who (I surmise) saw something of themselves as young men in him, and he succeeded in enlisting Franklin Roosevelt and Sam Rayburn as his patrons. Lyndon was a boy wonder in Texas politics through the blessing of these mentors and, in 1948, found himself running against Coke Stevenson in the democratic primary for U.S. senator. Before the campaign was over, according to Caro, Johnson had lied, cheated, and stolen many thousands of votes in a strategy cynical even by Texas standards; he showed himself to be without principle except for the one fundamental axiom that he must win. Johnson's greatest obstacle was the genuine kingliness of Coke Stevenson, and it was against this that Johnson's most shameless attacks were directed. In fact, it seems evident in reading Caro that Lyndon was fighting his own cynical shadow as he accused Coke of being an unprincipled "calculator" and a tool of special interests.

INDIAN DEMONS

Lyndon as a demon invites comparison with the classical Indian royal demons such as Vena, Duryodhana, Ravana, and Kamsa. Vena is especially apropos since, as Inden (1990) notes, Vena's "good" son Prthu is the archetypal king and the installation of every king involves overthrowing Vena in one form or another. Here is his story:

> King Vena's father had married the daughter of the god of Death, Yama. Because of the resultant "genetic" evil (*papman*) in his nature, Vena was born without faith in the gods and forbade his subjects to offer sacrifice to them. Vena disputed with the Brahmans about spiritual and philosophical issues, claiming that all six of their traditional orthodox "views" (*darsanas*) were false, and that the only true system was nihilism (*nastitva*). Vena went so far as to declare that the gods did not exist and that therefore all religious offerings (*puja*) should be made to him. The Brahmans were not pleased by this, and when their arguments and threats failed to change Vena's mind, they asked Vishnu to intervene. The god killed Vena by "churning" his thigh (a recognized means of procreation in Indian myths) and then his arm. From Vena's thigh was produced a dark-skinned aboriginal (*dasyu*), who embodied all Vena's evil, and from his arm came Prthu, the new king, who embodied the auspicious, dharmic qualities in Vena which had been suppressed by the evil ones. Prthu defeated the dasyu, banished him to the forests and wastelands outside his well-ordered kingdom, and inaugurated an age of manifest dharma on earth. King Vena himself was redeemed through these events and ascended to Indra's heaven. (*Harivamsa* 5)

King Vena is a pretentious parody of the cosmic man Purusa, and his blasphemous assertion of a right to receive the sacrifice mocks a famous line from the Rig Veda which says, "The gods sacrificed to sacrifice with sacrifice," meaning that Purusa (the human form of the sacrifice) was both the means and end of the sacrifice and also its material. That is, the origin, process, and aim of the ritual were identical; all were aspects of Purusa. King Vena identically asserts *aham iyajyas ca yasta ca yajnas ca:* "I am to be sacrificed to, I am the offerer of sacrifice and I am the sacrifice" (*Harivamsa* 5.7; see Heesterman 1985, p. 231n). The point of the story, of course, is that King Vena is wrong, while the Vedic sages were correct: Vena in truth only *participates* in Purusa (or Vishnu, who is Purusa's latter-day reflex), while Purusa encompasses all. Vena needs to be (as he becomes "in heaven" at the story's end) a "participant" in Vishnu, a *bhakta;* rather than a father, he needs to be a son.

The Vena/Prthu story, like all such tales in classical Indian culture, has a happy ending since the archetypal king, rooted in the god (Vishnu, Siva, etc.), necessarily overthrows the adharma of demons and others who oppose him. This is the King's nature and essential task. The ending was different in Texas in 1948 when Lyndon succeeded in masking his narcissistic amorality and in convincing the voters (or *almost* half of them) that he was the true "king" who would sweep away the self-centered old man Coke Stevenson and the "do nothing" disorder he supposedly represented. The demon was crowned when Lyndon took office. Today our politics turns on images of the King (and his Warrior, Wise Man and Father aspects), as it always has. The difference, which Robert Caro would trace partially back to 1948, is that politicians increasingly do not believe in the King but merely put on his costume and act the role. Near the front (as with Lyndon) or back of many politicians' minds is the cynicism of the demon king, often (as in our recent wars in Grenada, Panama, and Iraq) projected onto a convenient Other.[1]

---

1. Caro's book has recently generated a running confrontation in print with Jerome Blumenthal (*New York Times,* April 1, 1990), who criticizes Caro's idealization of Coke Stevenson and demonization of Lyndon. Whether or not Caro is justified in presenting Stevenson as such a complete expression of the good King, the essential point for my purposes is that Coke (like Robert Caro) was inspired and motivated by the king archetype and myth. Lyndon Johnson was motivated, as I think Caro clearly demonstrates, by the anti-king (or demon king) myth. I would suggest that Blumenthal's liberalism itself contains a large dose of anti-king mythology.

But this suggests that hunger for the King and Father in the collective consciousness is as strong as it has ever been and maybe stronger. Just as more fundamentalist ("stronger") forms of religion become attractive when God seems in danger of dissolving, so there has been a hunger for "stronger," ass-kicking leaders throughout the world in this century as the traditional structures of kingly order have been deconstructed by Westernization, secularization, and technology. The rub has been that many of our "kings" were rough beasts who did not believe in the King but, like Vena, put themselves in his place. They have been attractive to the masses but have generally been objects of ridicule to educated elites, although some of our greatest thinkers (Jung, Heidegger) have been deluded, by the depth of their awareness of our culture's need for the archetype, into validating them.

Who is destroying our King? I have no doubt that part of the answer is the eternal puer-senex split or (expressed somewhat differently) the conflict internal to the Fatherson, as one side or the other comes to its moment of self-assertion. But there must be more to it than this, for *neither* puer nor senex, Father nor Son, seems very credible these days. Throughout this book, I have tried to consider not only ego solutions to questions such as this, but also and especially archetypal ones. It is clear that the ego's (son's) hatred of the Father's world is as strong now as it has ever been, and that the "name of the father" is an F-word beyond the borders of post-structuralist France. Are *we* destroying him then? Is it just an oedipal paroxysm based on envy? But again, the inescapable question: *What is he doing to us?* I hear Lyndon's bitter disappointment in his father in this question, and my own hurt after my father was injured and after he died. We hate the Father because we cannot believe in him. The only answer, the only hope for us or him, is to save him, and the only way to do this is to understand his fall into weakness and tyranny and to see through both, not succumbing to the temptation to identify with either. This implies archetypal education, education in but also of the Father archetype, which is possible only as we accept our own mirroring and idealizing sonhood. We are still with the Indian king putting Prajapati together again, and thereby locating ourselves in our rightful places. Like Agni we are sons, but in being fully the Son, we, and Agni, are the Father's father, selfobjects to a new king whose kingdom will be more dharmic than the old.

BUDDHIST AND HINDU VIEWS
OF THE KING AND FATHERSON

As an Indianist in my "other" life (and to some extent in this book), I have often puzzled over the places of selfhood, the Fatherson, and the King in Buddhism. Unlike Vedic and Hindu religion, Buddhism has no place for "ultimate" kingly gods such as Varuna and Vishnu or the selfhood which they embody. The self itself is "empty" in Buddhism, and the Buddha spoke strongly against the Vedic religion, especially its human repository, the Brahman class. But in spite of the "no self" doctrine, which would seem to suggest a nonroyal view of society, Buddhism in fact supported and valorized the idea of the Chakravartin or world-ruling king, and Buddhist kings such as the Emperor Ashoka in fact lived up to the ideal more fully than any Hindu king before or since. The Buddha was himself of royal blood, and his mythology is filled with royal themes, such as the idea that his karma fitted him to be either a Buddha or a Chakravartin. The early Buddhist monuments called *stupas* were intended to represent the cosmos as centered on a relic of the Buddha which was enshrined at the center of an egg-shaped mound of stone; they are identical in meaning to the later Hindu temples which continuously represented the royal center of the world.[2] These stupas, and inscriptions on pillars preaching Buddhist ethics, were distributed throughout northern India as if they marked mileposts in a world-conquering "horse sacrifice."

The irony of a self-denying religion exalting the Great Man/ King, who generally represents the self writ large, seems to me intrinsically interesting but also heuristically useful. Although the issue of the nature of the Buddhist self far exceeds the aims of this book, the Buddhist effort to deny the self, in contrast to the Hindu

---

2. This is so also in the internal structure of both temple and stupa. As Inden (1990) shows, the Hindu temple (like Hindu reality generally) is organized so that its smaller, more interior parts are superior to and "encompass" its larger parts. Thus, the king is superior to his realm and "encompasses" it, for instance, because he is its source of life and structure (*dharma*). The image of the god in the temple's *sancta sanctorum* is superior to, and encompasses, the whole temple; the temple encompasses the remainder of the king's realm, etc. In the same way, the relic of the Buddha at the stupa's center is the seed from which the whole stupa (and the world it represents) has grown.

glorification of it, is a neat and suggestive way to look at our Fatherson data. This implies a criticism of the self deniers, and Obeyesekhere (1990, p. 241) notes that Buddhist "self"-denial has a "postmodern flavor" and provides a rubric in terms of which to view Western and Asian self-theories.

I have suggested that James Hillman's archetypal psychology lacks a self and, as a result, suffers from a hypertrophied anima. The other group of "no self" theorists reviewed here includes the poststructuralists or deconstructionists, particularly Lacan, Foucault, and Derrida and their followers. Both groups have a strong puer flavor, and we may note that the Buddha himself left the world of his father as a young man in a blaze of puer spirituality, abandoning his own wife and son, and had no future relationship with his own father (until the latter's death, when the Buddha returned to perform the funeral rites). The puer by himself is unstable, as Hillman has demonstrated, and needs his other half, the senex. Senex characteristics are not hard to locate in Buddhism: the very name of the Theravada school proclaims teachings "of the Elders." Although the Buddha has no significant relationship to his biological father or son, he is located within a lineage of other Buddhas who keep the Buddha dharma alive in successive ages of the world. These Buddhas are his functional fathers and sons, and we could also see the community of monks (sangha) as a patrilineal brotherhood.

Buddhism thus seems less "Buddhist" in its historical reality than deconstruction and archetypal psychology, but this may be an illusion caused by the newness of these movements. Let us look again for signs of the positive Fatherson in them. I suggested at the beginning of this chapter that deconstruction is erecting a king in disguise, a "hegemonic" "phallogocentric" father figure who reigns without title in the place of the cultural Fathers who preceded him and whom he seeks to overthrow. This idea has been argued by David Lehman (1990) in the case of Paul de Man, the eminent Belgian-American deconstructionist and past-life Nazi quisling. Lehman is good at exposing the adoration—sometimes genuine, sometimes fulsome—which much of the academic world had for de Man before his exposure and still has for de Man's guru, Jaques Derrida. Although the two are separated by a vast intellectual gulf, I view Lehman's de Man and Caro's Lyndon Johnson as brothers under the persona, two equally cynical applause-seekers able to manipulate the trappings of kingly generosity and nurturance of others while behind the veil furthering themselves with a steely purpose. But why did their disciples not see through the illusion to the manipulator Magician behind? One could equally ask, "Why didn't his subjects see through the Emperor's new clothes to his actual nakedness?" They failed to see the (absence of) clothes because they *did* see the Emperor (or rather, they saw the king archetype behind the actual emperor or through his imperfect, fading outer form). De Man's and Derrida's disciples see the Father behind the regicidal, depatriarchal rhetoric.

But this prompts a deeper reading of the de Man and Johnson "texts" and sheds light on the later career of James Hillman as well. Lehman notes Scott Fitzgerald's observation that "Gatsby sprang from his Platonic conception of himself" and asks, "Was this not true of Paul De Man?" (1990, p. 207). Although Lehman does not go anywhere with this idea, it points toward a way to reconcile the work and the life of de Man and Johnson, since, as even Lehman and Caro admit, not everything in their work was cynically purposed. Perhaps Johnson and de Man were guided by the Fatherson even as they consciously defamed him. The conscious (or foregrounded) half of the Fatherson for both Johnson and de Man—the "Platonic" image out of which each invented himself—was the abused and disappointed Son, perhaps in the mode of bully (in Robert Moore's terms) or revanchist. But in mocking and attacking the Father side of the archetype, de Man and Johnson may have acquired something of his nature, just as Indian demon "bhaktas" like Ravana achieve a closer union with the god through hatred than through love. In this way, we can account for the genuine affection felt for de Man's "pro-people" attitude by disciples and for Lyndon by many Texas Democrats even today: they see the King in these old Boys.

James Hillman, writing in *Spring* (1990), tackles another great American writer of the torn Fatherson, and specifically of sons seeking Father's initiation: Ernest Hemingway. In several of Hemingway's fictions, a dark mother figure and lover attacks the boy/man protagonist as he begins to establish a tie with the Father and so with his own male strength: this is the theme of "The Short Happy Life of Francis Macomber" and *The Garden of Eden,* the latter being the subject of Hillman's article. Hillman writes about Hemingway's novel about a writer, David Bourne, writing a story about hating his father and, in the writing, coming not (just) to hate him. The story is about hunting and killing an elephant, and Hillman's analysis is

Hindu rather than Buddhist: he sees the elephant as the elephant-headed god Ganesha and understands David's father problem *sub specie* the conflict and initiation between Ganesha and his god-father Siva. As always with Hillman, the end of the analysis is the *anima mundi* (although the word is not used here), but now there is more in that mundus than manifold species of flowers, each shining by its own, internal light. There is an *elephant:*

> a garden to be entered any evening when the bright mind cools, ourselves seated upon the elephant, swaying, sniffing the flowering ground, great foot lifted, paused in air. (1990, p. 112)

This elephant is the senex/Father, and in becoming the elephant's disciple, David deepens his sense of his own father. He finds (because he becomes able to accept) the Father's support.

> In the imagination of the sub-plot the boy has been initiated. He has left the father and returned to him. He has left simple resentment and found complex affection. He is no longer estranged from the fathering root, holding back from essential action, postponing, substituting. Woman also now shifts in his universe from wealthy supporter of his work to intimate partner in it. David finds the fathering capacity in his imaginative memory which he nourishes daily in the Africa of his mind, that high plateau where boy, father and elephant meet. The fiction of the father cures fixation on the father. (Ibid., p. 109)

Instead of being supported (kept) by his wealthy wife, David is now held by the elephant-Father "in his imaginative memory." In Fatherson terms, David has given up his effort to "be his own cause" as a man and has accepted the role of selfobject to the Father within, who as Hillman recognizes is also the distilled essence in memory of a lineage of actual fathers. The *tertium* which holds father and son together is the elephant, the imaginative fathering archetype which is infused with soul or anima.[3] The writer David (like the writer/narrator Ivan Karamazov) works to save his remembered father,

---

3. Or Fatherson archetype: Ganesha is a son, not a father, although he comes to participate in Siva's fatherhood by submitting to it as his *bhakta.*

fathering Father in learning to rest on him. The anima—self-objecthood herself as we concluded earlier—teaches this subtle way of being, this death in life or *esse in anima,* to David Bourne as she comes to him in the body of his new love Marita. David—his ego—has become an internal selfobject to the Father archetype, and the "fiction of the father" is fiction written *by* the Father but *through* his empirical son, David, and it "cures" not only David's "fixation" but his father's murderous lust to kill the elephant.

Although he has been working on this matter at least since his "Betrayal" piece (Hillman 1975), this is Hillman's most explicit acceptance of and submission to the Father in his published work. I am clearer now about why he has joined Bly in offering initiatory men's seminars: he seems more initiated himself.

CHAPTER 8

Initiating the Father Through Death

Whoever thinks He is killed, or thinks Him a killer, knows not: He does not kill and is not killed.

Bhagavad Gita *24.19*

When I was about nine, my dad (a hydrologist for the U.S. Geological Survey) took me into the belly of a dam. I had driven with him many times as he made his rounds collecting data, sitting in the truck while he retrieved ink-lined rolls of paper from the machines that recorded the rise and fall of rivers, and riding cable cars with him, our legs dangling above the brown swirl as he lowered bomb-shaped lead weights attached to instruments that measured the depth and speed of the stream below. I had inner-tubed and learned to swim in the warm summer rivers of northeastern Oklahoma as Dad waded nearby. But this morning was something different: Dad's friends in the Army Corps of Engineers were allowing him to take me down inside the Grand River dam. Dad and I drove an hour or two from home and parked beside the road, which continued on along the edge of a large lake. On its other side, the road was buttressed by the dam: a steep, concave cement wall at the bottom of which turbulent white water swirled into a reborn river.

We entered a cement box over the wall and descended in a slow elevator for a hundred feet or more to the bottom of the dam. A deep vibration, growing louder as we went down, did not prepare me for the misty cacophony that faced us when the elevator door opened. Below our feet a flood of water released from the lake's bottom leapt into the arms of squat, spinning turbines, a line of eight or ten of them emitting an agonized shriek of electric life. I felt (I now recognize) as I had on seeing, in the *Book of Knowledge,* rows of gods lining the narrow alleys of an Egyptian necropolis. We stepped to the cable-protected brink of the walkway, closer to the smooth dense curve of water that arced into the paddling turbine blades. I felt dizzy and deaf and held on to the cable as we watched foaming pools whirl ten feet from our eyes.

Toward his end a few years later, my father occasionally talked about life and death to me, but by then I wasn't much interested in him. The closest we ever came to a shared sense of life's depths and transience might have been that morning under the dam. I wonder, now, whether Dad took me so often to moving waters because he sensed their spiritual power, and whether his years of wading and floating in rivers gradually dissolved the hardness of ego in him and helped him face his approaching death. Did he unconsciously seek, by taking me inside the dam, an initiation for both of us?

I have tried to show in many contexts that initiation is a mutual affair: a father—or ritual elder—cannot initiate his son without, at the same time or later, undergoing initiation himself, and the initiatory *metanoia* of the son inevitably reflects back on the spiritual status of the father. Robert Bly reports that "an Australian aborigine said something to this effect: 'I've been doing this initiatory work with young men for forty years now, and I think I'm beginning to get it myself' " (1990, p. 233). But, we have also seen, the matter is not always viewed in this way, and the *father's* initiation remains tacit or incomplete in many rituals and literary discussions. Consciously, many classical and modern writers on initiation see the event as something done only for the *young* man's sake, a gift of spirit which flows from the older man's generative maturity but adds nothing to it; it can even seem to deplete the old man's already challenged vital essence. In this chapter, we will focus specifically on initiations that deal with the ultimate question, unavoidable for the older man, of death. Surely here, if anywhere, the Father's initiation must be the center of concern.

THE FATHER AND SON MOTIF IN THE BALDR MYTH

Initiation always involves some kind of "death" and rebirth into a new status. In a widely accepted formula, the initiate proceeds from his prior "ordinary" state (that of the "once born" in India) into a transitional or "liminal" condition where he is ritually dead, to a new status (in India that of the "twice born"). Prior to initiation one lives as a "boy," in Moore's terms; by contrast the initiated is a "man." As we have seen, however, boys and men struggle by nature for the single self they both crave and which, in essence, they both are. Often, from the man's viewpoint, the boy lacks respect for his elders, and initiation means taking the young man down a peg. This is the one-sided Oedipus/Laius view of the archetype, from which the older man must be rescued by undergoing his own complementary initiation. The "bad" father's initiation was one aspect of the Sunahsepa myth mentioned in the introduction.

Polomé's (1970) interpretation of the much-discussed Germanic myth of Baldr allows us to see the same issues at work. Baldr is the shiningly beautiful, sunlike son of the sovereign god Odin, begotten (in one version) on a mortal mother and beloved by all the gods. He is killed by his blind brother Hodr with a sprig of mistletoe and avenged the next day by his newborn brother Vali. Baldr's death is the event that leads to the catastrophe of Ragnarok, the destruction of the cosmos of the gods in a world battle where the dark forces are unchained and Odin himself is killed by his old foe, the Fenris wolf. Polomé argues that Hodr is, in fact, none other than a disguised form of father Odin—the master of disguises—himself, and that his killing of his son is an initiation of him parallel to that of the hero Haudebrand by his father Hildebrand (a form of Odin, following De Vries 1953). In killing Baldr, Odin would be initiating him to become one of his favorites, like the warriors Sigmund the Volsung and Harald Wartooth, both of whom Odin murdered and caused to join his band of warriors in Valhalla (Turville-Petre 1964, pp. 118-119).

Polomé argues that Baldr is killed by a plant symbolizing immortality—the evergreen mistletoe—precisely because Baldr himself *cannot* be immortal. Baldr's initiation represents a forced acceptance of mortality by presumptuous humankind: his initiation therefore requires a real death, not just a ritual one. This theme resonates with Greek religion, where the jealousy of the gods and their constant readiness to put down any sign of *hubris* is a primary motive in epic and tragedy.

There is no doubt that initiation often has this humiliating effect. The narcissism of the boy is brought low, and he is forced to recognize his submission to the "old block" from whom he came, a lower or partial form of whose nature he now takes on as his own. I have discussed this as the son's acceptance of mirroring self-objecthood toward the father. But there is another side to the matter, for if the son were nothing but a pale imitation of the father, there would be little of substance to be gained by the father, especially the divine father, in creating or engendering sons in the first place. Odysseus is initiated in his epic, passing through the many tests demanded by the god Poseidon, his baleful father figure who is reluctantly abetted by Zeus, the hero's paternal friend in heaven. But the long-suffering Odysseus is never completely humbled by the sea god. Indeed, it is clear that other gods, and especially Athena, admire Odysseus precisely *because* of his hubris, and Athena clearly expresses her pleasure at his wily plots. After listening to a full page of Odysseus's lies she praises him:

> The grey-eyed goddess smiled and stroked him with her hand.
> . . . "No one—not even if he were a god—could hope to dodge the plots that you concoct, unless he had consummate cunning, craft. Tenacious, shameless, driven to deceive, even in your own land you cannot leave behind the tales and traps, the lies you love." (Mandelbaum 1991, p. 273)

Even though there is evidence that the Greek gods do not entirely abhor the pride of their human sons, it is less clear that the gods themselves are ever initiated into a higher state of self-knowledge as a result of their encounters with men.[1] On the other hand, it could be argued that Greek tragedy and epic do wrestle with the fact that the gods *need* initiation, and that these texts express frustration at the powerlessness of men to make this happen. The Book of Job has been interpreted as homologous to a Greek tragedy, and certainly they share a similar theodicy, railing against God/gods for their refusal to care about the needs of men. Jung, in his *Answer to Job* (1952), asserts that Job succeeded in getting through to father God, who at least began an initiationlike process as a result of Job's prodding, a process which was continued in Christianity and later (implicitly) in analytical psychology (Stein 1985).

In the Baldr story, we do not directly see Odin develop, but if Polomé is right that Hodr is really *Odin,* then Vali's killing of Hodr is actually a killing of Odin, his older brother, and may represent a compensatory initiation of the god. Also, Odin's death at Ragnarok is to be followed by a new creation, and a new sovereign god, whom

---

1. But the "kingship in heaven" theme described by Scott Littleton (1970) may represent something of this kind. His idea is that the older, more brutal Greek divinities are brought low and superseded by their more "civilized" (we could say "more human") sons, as a consequence of the seniors' murderous actions toward them. Thus, Kronos can be understood as an initiated form of Uranus, Zeus as an initiated Kronos.

we may imagine as a reborn form of Odin himself. These questions are speculative, but the topic of Odin's initiatory self-sacrifice is well known and is indeed one of the most important and most mysterious issues in Germanic religion. Briefly, Odin hangs himself on the sacred world tree (Yggdrasil) for nine days and nights in quest of the sacred runes; in another episode, he blinds himself in one eye so that he can use it to see into the other world via the well of Mimir (see Sauvé 1970). Through this self-sacrifice, Odin attains immortality and omniscience. The key passage from the *Havamal* is this:

> I know that I hung on the windy tree for nine full nights, wounded with a spear and given to Odin, myself to myself; on that tree of which none know from what roots it rises. (Turville-Petre 1964, p. 42)

FATHERSON INITIATION IN THE *KATHA UPANISHAD*

Odin must initiate himself into the secrets beyond death because he has no son able to assist. I have argued elsewhere (Collins 1991a) that the ancient Indian story of Naciketas which frames the *Katha Upanishad* is about the initiation of a son, *and implicitly his father,* into a spiritual reality that transcends death. A middle-aged father, Vajasravasa, is afraid of his coming death and sacrifices all that he possesses in hopes of finding a solution. He sends his son, Naciketas—the name seems to mean "Ignoramus" or "Fool" (De Vries 1987), placing the boy in the folk-tale category of wise fool or "Dummling"—to the realm of King Yama, the god of death. Yama fails in his duty of hospitality toward the young Brahman, being absent for three days as Naciketas waits unfed. To make amends, Yama grants Naciketas three wishes, which taken together amount to the initiation of the boy, and through him of his father, so that both realize a Self beyond death.

Naciketas realizes that he has been sent to Yama to accomplish something for his father. The key verses suggest that this is initiation into the meaning of death:

> Naciketas to Vajasravasa: "What is to be done by Yama that [my father] will accomplish through me today?"

> Vajasravasa to Naciketas: "Reflect how it was in the past and
> anticipate that it will be so in the future: like grain a mortal
> ripens and like grain he sprouts again." (*Katha Upanishad*
> 1.1.5-6)

This is the father's level of insight before the initiation he seeks
from Yama: he knows the Brahmanic theory that the "self is born
from the self," the father emitting himself as seed which develops
into the son. Vajasravasa, however, is not satisfied with this accepted wisdom. He lacks the peace of mind (*santa-samkalpa*), happiness (*sumanas*), and freedom from anger (*vitamanyu*) towards his
son that Naciketas will seek for him with his first wish. Naciketas's
three wishes and Yama's fulfillments of them are:

> 1. That his father be free of anxiety, happy, and not angry with
> him. Yama assures him that his father will "sleep peacefully
> through the night, free from anger toward you."

> 2. To know the fire sacrifice that leads to heaven where there is
> no fear of old age or death. Yama describes the fire that is the
> "beginning of the world" and names it after Naciketas. He tells
> his pupil that by performing this sacrifice one "crosses over
> birth and death" and attains endless peace.

> 3. To know the answer to his (and his father's) deepest ques-
> tion: "There is a dispute about a departed man. Some say 'he
> is,' and others say 'he is not.' I would know this, instructed by
> you." Yama tries to buy Naciketas off with an offer of wealth
> and "as long a life as you want," but the boy insists, "the boon
> that penetrates the Mystery, no other than that does Naciketas
> choose." Finally, Yama instructs Naciketas in the paradoxical
> Self (*atman*) that exists before the opposites of birth and death,
> fear and peace, and father and son, and that makes it unneces-
> sary to rise via the sacrificial fire back to the origin of the world
> (the second wish).

The point of this series of wishes is, I think, to take the father beyond the old understanding that a self develops into a new
self (father into son) and to show him a selfhood ontologically prior
to both father and son. Paradoxically, the father can realize this
only through the efforts of his son. The old father–son relationship
had been poisoned by the father's terror of losing himself as his self
"flowed" into his son; this, I believe, was why father Vajasravasa

was angry (*manyu*) with Naciketas, and was the negative motiva-
tion for sending him to King Death. The third wish reveals a *tertium*
between and beyond father and son, heaven and earth, and death
and immortality. In realizing this transcendent truth the human
father Vajasravasa and his son Naciketas are also reconciled to each
other.

In Odin's story, and Naciketas's, death functions to strip
away illusions and show us a spiritual reality purified of the human
give and take, muddle and violence which Indian culture named
samsara, and which in India was evident perhaps above all in father–son conflicts. I argue that both of India's great epics, the
Ramayana and the *Mahabharata,* center on the need for evil "fathers" to be initiated and for "sons" to go beyond their bondage to
servitude of the "Laius" father and, in achieving their own selfhood,
to bring the old man also to the deeper self.

INITIATING THE DEMON/FATHER IN
THE *RAMAYANA* AND *MAHABHARATA*

Both of the great Indian epics are centrally "about" royal father–son
succession struggles. In "Rama's tale," the *Ramayana*—the most
popular story in Indian culture—the exemplary son and heir-appar-
ent Rama is deprived of kingship when his father, Dasaratha, con-
cedes to his junior wife Kaikeyi that her son Bharata will succeed to
his throne. The main line of the narrative deals with the consequences of Dasaratha's transgression and Rama's efforts to redeem
it. The encyclopedic *Mahabharata* contains many father–son (and
their equivalent, older brother–younger brother) succession rifts,
but the origin of most of them lies in one fateful event: Devavrata,
son of the last legitimate Kuru king Santanu, fails to become king
when he enables his father to marry a fishergirl, Satyavati, by accepting her condition that her son should become king after Santanu. In order to be confident that Devavrata will not interfere, she
further requires him to renounce his sexuality and remain celibate
for life. Devavrata will ever after be called "Bhisma," the "Awesome
One," because he readily agrees to this frightful vow.

In the course of the next two generations, matters go from
bad to worse as two factions of "sons" (actually nephews) struggle
for the kingship. Although his heart is with the "good" faction, the
Pandavas, Bhisma is the ally and chief warrior of the "evil" party,
the Kauravas or Dhartarastras. It is Bhisma's prowess as a warrior

that sustains the Dhartarastras and prevents a Pandava victory during the ten days of the war leading up to the crucial battle announced by the *Bhagavad Gita*. The task of restoring true kingship requires, above all, removing—i.e., killing—Bhisma, and returning him to his true nature; in a word, it means initiating him through death.

In the well known *"vishvarupa"* section of the *Bhagavad Gita* (chapter 33), where Krishna reveals his terrifying, cosmos-encompassing form to the Pandava brother Arjuna, we see Bhisma's initiation prefigured in Krishna's apotheosis. Arjuna is granted the vision of Bhisma, along with other father figures and finally the entire adharmic cosmos, being chewed up by Krishna's horrific mouths, reduced to formlessness, and reintegrated as part of Krishna's "supernal body" (*rupam aisvaram, Gita* 33.3). This involuntary "initiation" has the characteristic structure described by van Gennep (1960) and Turner (1969). In the *Gita* (33.25-40) the old forms are said to be crushed and ground (by Krishna's teeth), burned, or merged (like streams flowing into the ocean); thus they enter an amorphous liminal state and can be remolded into the shape of the Cosmic Man with whom Krishna is identified (*Gita* 33.39). Reduced to particulate formlessness by Krishna's eruption as a world-dissolving god, Bhisma and the lawless world which he epitomizes first become an almost Buddhist congeries of discrete elements, in the fullest sense what is called in Sanskrit a *visva* ("everything" without implied organization) as opposed to the *sarva* ("everything" considered as a unified whole) which they then enter as part of Krishna. In fact, these two words are significantly opposed in the *Gita*:

"All things (*visva*) are woven together on you." (*Gita* 33.38)

"I praise thee in front, I praise thee in back,
I praise thee on every side, O All! (*sarva*)
Of infinite vigor, of measureless might,
You encompass it all (*sarva*) and therefore are all (*sarva*). (*Gita* 33.40, van Buitenen 1981)

The items of the world are made a whole, a *sarva,* by being woven like discrete strings of a carpet into the preexisting warp of Krishna.

The three stages of the initiation, then, are 1) the old form (the existing kingship of Dhrtarastra and Bhisma's support for it), 2) a liminal state (old kingship ground up into a *"visva"* by Krishna), and 3) the new form (Krishna's supernal form and its representative on earth, a renewed Kuru kingship which integrates the world as a "*sarva*").

"Release" (*moksa*) in Indian thought usually involves the "recycling" of old, defective forms—their state of being is often described by metaphors of constraint or *bondage*—back into the body of the Cosmic Man. A little later in the *Gita,* Bhisma states that he has been "bound" (*baddha*) or "enslaved" (*hrta*) by the "*artha*" of the Kauravas. He explains that "man is the slave of *artha*, but *artha* is the slave of no man" (*arthasya puruso daso tv artho na kasyacit, Gita* 41.36). Van Buitenen translates the multivalanced word *artha* (literally "aim" or "object") as "wealth," but I suggest the sense is rather that man, in this instance Bhisma, is bound by taking *artha*, in its usual sense of "the seeking of personal advantage," as his chief motive. In this interpretation, *artha* would be equivalent to the pursuit of the *Bhagavad Gita's* favorite *bete noire*, "the fruits of action" (*karmaphala*). Bhisma is tragically entangled in the advantage-seeking of others in his patrilineage: in the first place, his own father's lust for Satyavati; later the self-seeking of Dhrtarastra's sons. His release from *artha* bondage requires that he be ground up and made part of the new dharma being brought about by son figures, Krishna and the Pandavas.

Initiation of the Father through death is also the central theme of the *Ramayana,* although fatherhood in the shorter epic is displaced for the most part onto cosmic demons, in particular the archdemon of Indian culture, Ravana (the monster who steals Rama's wife Sita and takes her to be his queen in Ceylon). This is a familiar theme in India, and a number of famous demons have been cited (in chapters 6 and 7)—Bali, Vena, etc.—who are, in effect, pretenders to the throne of the archetypal father and who are overthrown for their inflation and reduced to the status of de facto sons, i.e., devotees of the god who defeats them. In Ravana's case, it seems clear that the demon is implicitly identified with Rama's father and that, in killing Ravana, Rama overcomes and renews his own father.

For the most part, Rama functions in Indian popular religious thought as the ideal initiated or "twice born" son, because he subordinates himself so totally to his father's wishes. I argue the converse, that implicitly Rama must and does overcome, defeat, and even kill his father so that the *old man* can be initiated. In the Sanskrit *Ramayana* (the earliest full telling of the story), and even more pointedly in later, vernacular retellings, Ravana becomes a devotee of Rama at the moment of his death (often being revealed as already a devotee in a past life) and merges into Rama's divine essence as he passes away.

Because fathers' views tend to be culturally hegemonic, many stories minimize older men's need for initiation at and through death and for the help of their sons. Nevertheless, the need is real and shows the defensive core and inherent self-contradiction of patriarchal consciousness—as it is named by those who take the "strong" masculine at its own daytime valuation. At bottom, self-sacrifice and death are essential to the patriarchy, as Father flows into Son and again, momentarily, finds himself.

CHAPTER 9

Toward an Archetypal Self Psychology

Kohut's idea of the selfobject (discussed in chapter 2) and Hillman's idea, after Jung and the Platonic tradition, of an *anima mundi* (discussed in chapters 1 and 4) represent two landmarks in the long return to Western consciousness of a self–world nondualism. What emerges for both thinkers is not a holism or monism but rather a continual or repeated discovery of the self in the world, or—in privative mode—disclosure of its absence there. Conversely, there is a discovery of the world in the self (or what had been thought to be a wholly internal, undivided self). Hillman and Kohut complement one another when viewed from this perspective. Kohut does not seriously question Western individualism, and so his self is confined to the person ("body–mind self" or "nuclear self") and the selfobject realm is to be found only "outside," in the environment. Moments of self–world nonduality are therefore few and special, being mainly confined to our most intimate relationships and dearest goals. Self-selfobject appropriateness is something sought by the self and to a large extent made to happen by it. Kohut thus privileges the self side of the relation.[1] Hillman, on the other hand, has no use for the Western individual (the "heroic ego"). For him, selfhood is no more the prerogative of persons than it is of flowers and stones or, for that matter, of complexes and archetypes. He tends to lose or blur the essential self-selfobject distinction and fall into a pan-selfobject monism, which he accurately describes as "animism."

Because Kohut for the most part does not question the basic unity of the "body-mind self," the issue of selfobjects *internal* to the person is not usually salient for him: all selfobjects are part of the environment and somatic and psychological parts of the person are not understood as selfobjects.[2] We saw, however, that his theory

---

1. In his last writings, Kohut seems to move toward more trust in the selfobject, and a greater degree of accepting reliance on it.

2. It is generally recognized that self psychologists waffle on the issue of whether selfobjects are internal or external. The question is essentially irrelevant from the perspective taken here: whether they are inside or outside, selfobjects are always coded as "environmental." There is a felt

does implicitly have room for the idea of an internal selfobject, since in fact the model for all selfobjects is the sense of ownership and control we have over our (presumably internal) bodies and minds. The fact that this control is not absolute implies that there is always a felt difference between selfhood as such and body/mind self, and that the latter is best understood as consisting of more or less appropriate selfobjects. But having opened this door, it seems only natural to look for inner selfobjects beyond the body, the conscious, and even the personal unconscious psyche. Archetypal contents of the psyche such as anima, Mother, and Fatherson may be the most important selfobjects, those most productive of self-sense and most able to diminish it.

We found that Kohut's theory also implies a self-selfobject reciprocity or mutuality. Diachronically, the self at one moment becomes the selfobject at a later time, and the former selfobject comes into its own selfhood; synchronically viewed, self is also selfobject and selfobject is self. It was this insight that led me to read the Father and Son archetypes as the nondual Fatherson. Adding this realization to our expanded self psychology, we have *reciprocal internal* selfobject relationships such as those between Father and Son, and between ego and anima. Viewing the relations among archetypes as selfobject relationships, we are in a better position to see how selfhood inheres in each archetype, but also seemingly shifts from one archetype to another in the "play of consciousness." I have suggested that active imagination is essentially just this shifting self-selfobject sport. Furthermore, through the diachronic play—and strife—of the inner selfobject world a *coniunctio* is achieved and an essence distilled out of the psyche's "history."

We have used the Fatherson as an extended example of this psychic playing with oneself that is not onanism. Seeing the Father archetype in a syzygy with the Son, we sons (all men) are freed to

---

difference of nature between body and mind (felt as "inside") and internal representations of the self-relevant environment (felt as "outside"). Ambitions and ideals, the constituents of the "nuclear self," exist in an ambiguous status since they are conceived as parts of the self but develop from (environmental) selfobjects (i.e., mirroring and idealized parts of the environment). This ambiguity, along with the process of "transmuting internalization" whereby selfobjects become self, has been seen by others as a weakness of Kohut's theory. Perhaps the problematic nature of this area of his thought was a motive in Kohut's decision to downplay internalization in his late work.

learn from the father but also to see his failings and to act to save him as we would want him to save us. We have seen a number of holes into which the old man can fall, among them those of the buffoon and the demon (or tyrant). As we get beyond the immature perspective that selfhood is a good of limited quantity and that we must fight the Father (or Son) to take away his share, it becomes clear that to be Father or Son at all (or at least "in fullness"), we must serve and save the other, which can sometimes mean fighting him in order to return him to his dharma, as do the avatars of Vishnu and the kings who share their nature. Conversely, in an idealizing mode, we must allow ourselves to be purged of evil by "participation" *(bhakti)* in the greater truth of a divine Father.

The fact of internal selfobjects, particularly archetypal ones, gives us a new perspective on external selfobjects such as idealized parent figures and mirroring friends and lovers, which for Kohut were the only selfobjects. I believe that the notion of selfobjects within the psyche allows us to dissolve the subject-object barrier and to understand the inside-outside opposition as really being an aspect of a more fundamental self-selfobject distinction which itself, as I hope to have shown, is not an opposition at all but a creative and self-sacrificial inherence.[3] This is a subtle point, and it is easy to get lost in the various failed solutions we have reviewed, particularly the demonic one which would see the whole world as only a part of the ego self. Let me return again to *"hantaham!"*, the Vedic utterance of "I" in which Prajapati finds himself through sacrifice. As I have argued, following Indian thought, the finding of a selfobject requires an ontologically earlier self-sacrificial "flowing out" (in Sanskrit, a *srsti*) of the self in the form of a body, mind, or utterance—in our example, the word "I."[4] This creative or emanational moment for the (primordial) self develops into a moment of grace or perhaps of brute "thrownness" for the selfobject to which it gives life; it is this second moment that constitutes the particular nature or "suchness" *(tathata)* of the things of the world, including the ego which, in terms

---

3. Jung's intense interest late in life in the psychic nature of matter and synchronicity moved in the same direction (see Jung 1951, par. 261).

4. Jung discusses this process in terms of Meister Eckhart's thought on the divine Fatherson: "Only the Father, the God 'welling' out of the Godhead, 'notices himself,' becomes 'beknown to himself,' and 'confronts himself as a Person.' So, from the father, comes the Son, as the Father's thought of his own being" (Jung 1959, p.193).

of the *hantaham,* is more "I" than I. The third moment of this nexus is the self-selfobject mutuality or *coniunctio* which takes place as the selfobject dissolves back into the self, becoming at this moment fully its selfobject (i.e., reflecting back the self to itself): "I am 'I'," where the "I"-word "fades" into the I-self.

In terms of Indian cosmogonic theories, and the subset of these ideas which constitute the theory of kingship, the internal dynamism of the self-selfobject process implies a particular sort of cosmos and personal world. The world, at whatever level, is organized around a self which is both losing itself and finding itself in its world. As we saw in an earlier discussion, each "world," whether that of a poor farmer or a world king, is a *kula* or "family," and at its center is a person who is its self. The essential task of a king, or of a father/patriarch, is to maximize the "finding self" side of the process and minimize the chaotic disorganization which follows the entropic loss of self. But it is just here that the demonic possibility lies, for if, like King Vena, a person demands that the world devote itself wholly to mirroring him (as Vena does in trying to become his subjects' sole object of worship), he loses the self-selfobject distinction and falls into a merger: he becomes a King Midas who has also turned himself to gold. Things are indeed well organized for such a king (his trains run on time), but they are no longer creative, there is no possibility of new life. This is why the Indian cosmos, as imagined in classical Hindu thought, always posits a deeper self upon which the self of a given *kula* rests. Behind the regional king is a world king (*cakravartin*); behind the world king is Vishnu. As we see in exquisite detail in Kashmiri Shaivism, even within God there are levels of depth, and the divine self at a more superficial (*saguna*) level rests on a deeper, unmanifest (*nirguna*) self. Demons are those "kings" who forget that they rest on, and are mirroring selfobjects for, more encompassing kings.[5]

---

5. Or rest on, and mirror, the Goddess. Although we are placing the Fatherson solution in the foreground here, Indian mythology also places the Goddess in the role of the always-deeper divine background to any given "king." When the Goddess slays the buffalo demon Mahisha, she defeats an overweening male pride (the male buffalo signifies virility), but in a specifically feminine way. The kingly buffalo seeks the Goddess as his sexual partner, in this way attempting to turn the entire earth,

The philosopher Ramanuja notes that "demons" believe they are the cause of their own world (van Buitenen 1953, pp. 155-158). Wise men do not believe that they are the cause even of their own bodies and minds. Paradoxically, at the very instant of creative emanation the self's agent force enters (becomes) the selfobject, which henceforth is the sole power (*sakti*) in the world. The demonic attempt to hold onto and direct the *sakti* is bound to fail and, in fact, ironically condemns the one who tries it to lose selfhood even faster, becoming an ever more material, grosser selfobject to the (residual) God, who in one way or another will put him in his place. Accepting that *sakti* acts, not I, one allows oneself to be an idealized selfobject to the emanated self "material," which naturally seeks to mirror its origin: this is the dance of *prakrti* before *purusa*. In the end, only the selfobject acts; the self is passive, and the true king—in his essential or highest nature—replicates the tantric image of Siva lying dead, although like Osiris with phallus creatively erect, under the Goddess who is *sakti*. The king acts indeed, but in acting dharmically he sacrifices himself ("forward") into the fire of his action and simultaneously releases himself ("backwards") into the God who stands motionless behind him. The fire of action is *sakti,* who—because she flows from the God/self, and recalls her tie with him—is soul (anima) and the essential selfobject, and all selfobjects partake of her. As Hillman says, "[Anima] is the psychic factor in nature" (1985, p. 23). I would only add that she is also the *self* factor, or, better, the flavor (*rasa*) of selfhood.

Thus, whether they are inside or outside the "body-mind self" is irrelevant to the nature of selfobjects. Whatever mirrors the self is a selfobject and what does not mirror, or positively detracts from, a positive sense of self is not a selfobject (or in my terms is a "bad" selfobject). Starting from the selfobject perspective, in fact, we can suggest that the concepts of "internal" and "external" derive from

---

which she represents, into his selfobject. The Goddess attracts Mahisha with her beauty and then beheads him, symbolically (and sometimes explicitly) castrating him and cutting off his pretensions of mastery via literal "phallocentrism." The Goddess is sometimes represented as encompassing the three worlds (heaven and midspace in addition to the earth), thus paralleling Vishnu as he overcomes the demon King Bali (see Dimmitt and van Buitenen, 1978, p. 238).

the general experience that "good" selfobjects tend to be found within the body and mind, the family circle, the ethnic group, one's native place, etc. "Outside" is that part of the environment where "bad" selfobjects are mostly located.[6]

THE SELF SQUARED AND
THE ORDER OF SELFOBJECTS

As we saw earlier, Kohut posits three types of selfobjects: mirroring, idealized, and twin. The origins within psychoanalysis of the first two are easy to see: the mirroring selfobject represents a reinterpretation of the preoedipal and especially oral experience of the infant, while idealized selfobjects are a theoretical transformation in self psychology of the Freudian Oedipus complex as successfully resolved. This is why mirroring selfobjects are naturally associated with maternal figures and idealized ones with paternal. I suggested that the motive for the twin selfobject was Kohut's nonconscious wish to combine the mirroring and idealized types into a reciprocal, conjunct, and nondual selfobject dyad, and I have followed this approach in my discussion. But it would not do to ignore the meat of classical psychoanalysis and Jungian thought, the drives, complexes, and archetypes. This is one reason I have approached the Fatherson as a specific flavor of self and selfobjecthood. There are other flavors, of course, and we have seen that there are a number of them even within the Fatherson itself (buffoon, demon, weakling, dharmic king, senex, puer, teacher, etc.). The only other archetypes we have discussed are two feminine ones: anima and Mother, both in terms of Father–Son relations. It would be possible to construct a more complete archetypal self psychology, one with many more fla-

---

6. There has been, since the Renaissance and particularly in the Romantic movement, a dramatic shift in the Western (Christian) sense of the moral or feeling value of wild nature; what had been experienced mostly as a frightening, alien, and antispiritual presence has now become (at least in fantasy) a loving Mother and a place of cleansing purity. Perhaps this change involves seeing nature as a negative selfobject, a place to realize that our shopping-mall civilization is not a proper selfobject for us. But there is also a return to an earlier, pre-Christian, sense of oneness with nature which has been preserved, for example, in the the "Green Man" image (Anderson and Hicks 1990).

vors of selfobject and a more complex structure. Although doing this in any detail clearly lies outside my intentions here, I cannot resist a *sumii* sketch of the project.

Robert Moore, following Jung's *Aion,* imagines the archetypal psyche as two pyramids base to base, or a "double quaternio," one representing masculine psychology, one feminine psychology. Building on this image, and without discussing the alchemical particulars of Jung's ideas, I will look again at the ego-self question as Jung saw it and try to show how various psychic flavors can be understood to flow from this fundamental relation.

Jung never tired of telling us that the ego is the "center of the field of consciousness" and that the center of the larger psyche is the self. To relativize the ego is to allow it to become a "content" of a higher, *self* consciousness (or to recognize that the ego is *already* a content of the self). The idea of the "objective psyche" tells us that for Jung *all* the contents of the psyche are selfobjects, and it might be better, after Kohut, to call it the "selfobject psyche." But this clearly shows that the totalizing Jungian self implies a kind of essential selfhood from which all the selfobject archetypes arise, and to which they point: the center of the *mandala.* "Ego" would more properly designate the demonic tendency inherent in each of the archetypes to *deny its own selfobjecthood* (its participation in the objective psyche) and to *presume autonomy as self* toward some other psychic content which would be its selfobject. In this sense, ego would be an intrinsic attribute of all archetypes, at least as they are lived in the form of personal complexes striving for self-expression or power.

The first move of a primordial male self letting itself flow into a selfobject world is imagined in India and in the West in two primary ways: as a man seeks a wife, and as a father seeks a son. The first possibility leads to the *coniunctio* of the King and Queen, the second to the Fatherson. With Indian cosmogony, we can see the process as twofold: an emissional or emanational first phase (*pravrtti*) is followed by a second, involutional or reconstitutive phase (*nivrtti* or *unmesa*). The archetypes of the second phase would be the *anima* and the *puer,* respectively. While both phases are both self and selfobject to one another, the first phase places the self as agent in the foreground and the second the patient selfobject. Actively manifesting self, the primordial male falls immediately into selfobjecthood; accepting selfobjecthood, his emitted alter ego paradoxically finds himself again. Negative possibilities are inherent in this pattern: refusing a supportive player's role, the emitted creature may turn demon and rouse the original being to a warrior's wrath to compel order in the world. As tyrant, the original male may refuse the selfobject-son enough room and anger him to become oedipal castrator, "opener" of the serpent that binds his world shut.

Viewing the original self as female, we might imagine a similar twofold initial impulse of seeking a selfobject: first, as mother she would seek her daughter, whom we will call the *kore,* following Jungian tradition (Jung and Kerenyi 1969; Neumann 1954).[7] Second, as Great Mother (or Queen), she would seek the young, "dying" god, her husband/son, whom we would name *Attis,* again following the tradition. The second half of the process, the return toward the originating self, is not as clear to me as in the masculine case, but I suggest we could see the kore's return via Hades, the god of death who takes her away from the Mother but also brings her back each year. The return of Attis is not a problem, since he dies almost before he is born and seems to lack the degree of individuation or distance from the self necessary to be a proper selfobject. In his case the separation/rapprochement process requires increasing distance or conscious objectivity, and I suggest that the agent of this consciousness might be the animus. Negative possibilities in the feminine cycle would include the hero as a compensatory development of the Attis figure who refuses to return as the Mother-self's selfobject, and, in the Kore's case, the sort of girl who becomes an anima woman for men and neglects her tie to the Mother archetype (cf Jung and Kerenyi 1969, p. 172). Parallel to the male tyrant, the female can become a smothering witch who will not let her son or daughter get far enough away to become selves in their own right.

The masculine paths have been explored by James Hillman, who seems temperamentally more comfortable with the male realm, while developments from the feminine perspective were the favored territory of Erich Neumann. Jung himself worked along both lines of thought but initially leaned toward development out of the femi-

-----

7. Kerenyi understands the mother goddess Demeter and her daughter Persephone as one complex personality, quite similar to my conception of the Fatherson. He quotes an inscription that identifies the goddess as both maiden (kore) and mature woman (gyne) and sees the Eleusinian mysteries as turning on the mother-daughter identification (Jung and Kerenyi 1969, p. 181).

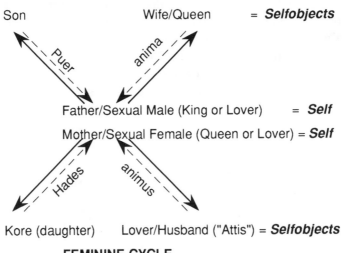

MASCULINE CYCLE

Son   Wife/Queen   = *Selfobjects*

Father/Sexual Male (King or Lover)   = *Self*

Mother/Sexual Female (Queen or Lover) = *Self*

Kore (daughter)   Lover/Husband ("Attis") = *Selfobjects*

FEMININE CYCLE

nine, with emphasis on the hero myth as the origin of ego conscious-ness. He seems to have moved in his later years toward a greater interest in the masculine cycle.

What I hope to have gained in writing this book, and what I would wish its readers to take from it, is an enhanced capacity for Fatherson meditation, a greater sense of the "calmness" (Kohut's excellent word, which Moore also uses) we sons can touch in holding the larger hand of the man who stands beside us in life, even—or especially—after his physical death.

I recall again swimming in the rivers of northeastern Oklahoma as my dad waded nearby, measuring their flow; cleaning a lotus pond while Gurudev watched; working on a dream as my ana-lyst listened. The presence of the Father with us but letting us be, finding himself without using us up, is one of the most com-forting things in the world for sons. Because of his calm reality I can now work as a therapist with men and hug my son without the strain of needing them too much or fearing that they will be stifled by my expectations. I can also see that my love for my Father must be active, that I must work to save him from the chaos and banality into which he falls without me. For me, it is a beautiful paradox that only through resting on the Father can I find the strength to save him. Let me end by allowing Dad to carry me once more, in imagination, as he did in my personal history at age six when we moved from my birthplace to Pryor, Oklahoma. Riding with him in the government panel truck (my brother and mother were in the family car), I recall my blocked sadness as we drove out of town. Dad caught my mood and spoke to me, "Say good-bye to Oklahoma City, son." His empathy helped me to cry and then to fall asleep on the seat beside him.

BIBLIOGRAPHY

Aitareya Brahmana. 1863. Edited by M. Haug. Bombay: Government Central Book Depot. Citations translated by the author.

Anderson, W., and Hicks, C. 1990. *Green Man: The Archetype of Our Oneness with the Earth.* London: HarperCollins.

Bacal, H. A. 1990. Does an object relations theory exist in self psychology? *Psychoanalytic Inquiry* 10:197–220.

Beck, B. E. F., Claus, P. J., Goswami, P., and Handoo, J. 1987. *Folktales of India.* Chicago: University of Chicago Press.

Bettelheim, B. 1977. *The Uses of Enchantment: The Meaning and Importance of Fairy Tales.* New York: Knopf.

Bloom, H. 1973. *The Anxiety of Influence.* Oxford University Press.

Bly, R. 1990. *Iron John: A Book about Men.* Reading, Mass.: Addison Wesley.

Boer, C. 1970. *The Homeric Hymns.* Dallas: Spring Publications.

Brhadaranyaka Upanishad. In *The Principal Upanishads,* S. Radhakrishnan, ed. London: Allen and Unwin, 1962. Citations translated by the author.

Caro, R. 1990. *The Years of Lyndon Johnson,* vol. 2, *Means of Ascent.* New York: Vintage.

Carstairs, M. 1967. *The Twice Born: A Study of a Community of High-Caste Hindus.* Bloomington, Ind.: Indiana University Press.

Chodorow, N. J. 1978. *The Reproduction of Mothering.* New Haven, Conn.: Yale University Press.

Collins, A. 1975. Reflections on RV X.129. *Journal of Indo-European Studies* 2:271–281.

——. 1976. The origins of the Brahman-king relationship in Indian social thought. Ph.D. dissertation. University of Texas at Austin.

———. 1991a. Sunahsepa and Akanandun. In M. Stein and L. Corbett, eds. *Psyche's Stories: Jungian Interpretations of Fairy Tales.* Wilmette, Ill.: Chiron Publications.

———. 1991b. From Brahma to a blade of grass: Indian cosmogony and the self. *Journal of Indian Philosophy* 19:143–189.

———. 1991c. For Purusa's sake: Psychoanalytic self psychology and the metaphysics of selfhood in three Indian philosophies, part 1. *The Mankind Quarterly* 32:19–42.

———. 1993. Men within: Robert Bly, *Iron John: A Book about Men;* Robert Moore and Douglas Gillette, *King Warrior Magician Lover: Rediscovering the Archetypes of the Mature Masculine;* Robert Moore and Douglas Gillette, *The King Within: Accessing the King in the Male Psyche.* Reviewed in *The San Francisco Jung Institute Library Journal* 11:17–32.

Collins, A., and Desai, P. 1986. Selfhood in context: Some Indian solutions. In *The Cultural Transition,* M. I. White and S. Pollak. eds. New York: Routledge and Kegan Paul.

Colum, P., ed. 1972 *The Complete Grimm's Fairy Tales.* New York: Pantheon.

Devereux, G. 1953. Why Oedipus killed Laius: A note on the complementary Oedipus complex in Greek drama. *International Journal of Psychoanalysis* 34:132–141.

De Vries, L. 1987. The father, the son and the ghoulish host: A fairy tale in ancient Sanskrit? *Asian Folklore Studies* 46:227–256.

Dimmitt, C., and van Buitenen, J. A. B. 1978. *Classical Hindu Mythology.* Philadelphia: Temple University Press.

Dodds, E. R. 1966. *The Greeks and the Irrational.* Berkeley, Calif.: University of California Press.

Eggeling, J. 1900. *The Satapatha Brahmana,* 5 parts. Oxford: Clarendon Press.

Ellenberger, H. 1970. *The Discovery of the Unconscious.* New York: Basic Books.

Frankfort, H. 1948. *Kingship and the Gods*. Chicago: University of
    Chicago Press.

Freud, S. 1900. *The Interpretation of Dreams*. *SE*, vol. 5. London:
    Hogarth Press.

——. 1911. Formulations regarding the two principles in mental
    functioning. In *Freud: General Psychological Theory*, M. N.
    Searl trans. New York: Collier Books.

——. 1939. Analysis terminable and interminable. *SE*, vol. 23. London:
    Hogarth Press.

Gallop, J. 1985. *Reading Lacan*. Ithaca, N.Y.: Cornell University Press.

Gendlin, E. 1985. Some notes on the "self." *The Focusing Folio* 4(4):136–
    151.

——. 1987. A philosophical critique of the concept of narcissism: The
    significance of the awareness movement. In *Pathologies of the
    Modern Self: Postmodern Studies on Narcissism, Schizophrenia,
    and Depression*, D. M. Levin, ed. New York: New York
    University Press.

Gilligan, C. 1982. *In a Different Voice*. Cambridge, Mass.: Harvard
    University Press.

Goldman, R. 1978. Fathers, sons and gurus: Oedipal conflict in the
    Sanskrit epics. *Journal of Indian Philosophy* 6:325–392.

Gonda, J. 1966a. *Ancient Indian Kingship from the Religious Point of
    View*. Leiden: E. J. Brill.

——. 1966b. *Loka: World and Heaven in the Veda*. Amsterdam: N. V.
    Noord- Hollandsche Uitgevers Maatschappij.

Grinnell, R. 1970. Reflections on the archetype of consciousness. *Spring*
    1970:15–39.

Hanly, P., and Masson, J. M. 1976. A critical examination of the new
    narcissism. *International Journal of Psychoanalysis* 57:49–66.

*Harivamsa. The Mahabharata: Text as Constituted in its Critical
    Edition*, vol. 5. Poona: The Bhandarkar Oriental Research
    Institute, 1975. Citations translated by the author.

Heesterman, J. C. 1985. *The Inner Conflict of Tradition: Essays in Indian Ritual, Kingship and Society.* Chicago: University of Chicago Press.

Hillman, J. 1968. Senex and puer: an aspect of the historical and psychological present. *Eranos Jahrbuch 1967.* Zurich: Rhein Verlag.

———. 1972. *The Myth of Analysis.* Evanston, Ill.: Northwestern University Press.

———. 1973. The Great Mother, her son, her hero and the puer. In *Mothers and Fathers,* P. Berry, ed. Dallas: Spring Publications.

———. 1975. *Loose Ends: Primary Papers in Archetypal Psychology.* Zurich: Spring Publications.

———. 1979a. *The Dream and the Underworld.* New York: Harper and Row.

———. 1979b. *Puer Papers.* Dallas: Spring Publications.

———. 1983a. *Inter Views: Conversations with Laura Pozzo on Psychotherapy, Biography, Love, Soul, Dreams, Work, Imagination and the State of the Culture.* New York: Harper and Row.

———. 1983b. *Archetypal Psychology: a Brief Account.* Dallas: Spring Publications.

———. 1983c. *Healing Fiction.* Barrytown, N.Y.: Station Hill Press.

———. 1985. *Anima: An Anatomy of a Personified Notion.* Dallas: Spring Publications.

———. 1990. The elephant in the Garden of Eden. *Spring* 50:93–115.

Homans, P. 1979. *Jung in Context: Modernity and the Making of a Psychology.* Chicago: University of Chicago Press.

Inden, R. 1990. *Imagining India.* Oxford: Blackwell.

Inden, R., and Nicholas, R. 1977. *Kinship in Bengali Culture.* Chicago: University of Chicago Press.

Irigaray, L. 1985. *Speculum of the Other Woman*. Ithaca: Cornell University Press.

Joseph, S. 1987. Review of Jaques Lacan's *Écrits. The San Francisco Jung Institute Library Journal* 7(2):1–16.

Jung, C. G. 1954. Archetypes of the collective unconscious. In *CW* 9i:3–41. Princeton, N.J.: Princeton University Press, 1959.

——. 1951. *Aion. CW,* vol. 9ii. Princeton, N.J.: Princeton University Press.

——. 1955–1956. *Mysterium Coniunctionis. CW ,* vol. 14. Princeton, N.J.: Princeton University Press, 1963.

——. 1946. The psychology of the transference. In *CW* 16:163–326. Princeton, N.J.: Princeton University Press, 1966.

——. 1931. The nature of the psyche. In *CW* 8:159–234. Princeton, N.J.: Princeton University Press, 1960.

——. 1952. *Answer to Job*. In *CW* 11:355–470. Princeton, N.J.: Princeton University Press, 1969.

Jung, C. G., and Kerenyi, K. 1969. *Essays on a Science of Mythology*. Princeton, N. J.: Princeton University Press.

Katha Upanishad. In *The Principal Upanishads,* S. Radhakrishnan, ed. London: Allen and Unwin, 1962. Citations translated by the author.

Kierkegaard, S. 1955. *Fear and Trembling / Sickness unto Death*. W. Lowrie, trans. Garden City, N.Y.: Doubleday.

Knipe, D. 1977. Sapindikarana: The Hindu rite of entry into heaven. In *Religious Encounters with Death,* F. E. Reynolds and E. H. Waugh, eds. Philadelphia, Penn.: Pennsylvania State University Press.

Kohut, H. 1959. Introspection, empathy and psychoanalysis. In *Search for the Self: Selected Writings of Heinz Kohut,* P. Ornstein, ed. New York: International Universities Press, 1978.

——. 1971. *The Analysis of the Self*. New York: International Universities Press.

——. 1977. *The Restoration of the Self.* New York: International
        Universities Press.

——. 1984. *How Does Analysis Cure?* Chicago: Univ. of Chicago Press.

Kohut, H., and Wolf, E. 1978. The disorders of the self and their
        treatment: An outline. *International Journal of Psychoanalysis*
        59:413–425.

Lacan, J. 1960. The subversion of the subject and the dialectic of desire
        in the Freudian unconscious. In *Lacan* Écrits: *A Selection,* A.
        Sheridan, trans. London: Tavistock, 1977.

Larson, G. J. 1969. *Classical Sankhya.* Delhi: Motilal Banarsidass.

——. 1980. Karma as a "sociology of knowledge" or "social psychology" of
        process/praxis. In *Karma and Rebirth in Classical Indian
        Traditions,* W. D. O'Flaherty, ed. Berkeley: University of
        California Press.

Lehman, D. 1991. *Signs of the Times: Deconstruction and the Fall of
        Paul de Man.* New York: Poseidon Press.

Lévi-Strauss, C. 1969. *The Elementary Structures of Kinship.* Boston:
        Beacon Press.

Lipner, J. 1986. *The Face of Truth. A Study of Meaning and
        Metaphysics in the Vedantic Theology of Ramanuja.* Albany:
        SUNY Press.

Lipsey, R., ed. 1977. *Coomaraswamy: Selected Papers,* vol. 2:
        Metaphysics. Princeton, N.J.: Bollingen Series, Princeton
        University Press.

Littleton, C. Scott. 1966. *The New Comparative Mythology: An
        Anthropological Assessment of the Theories of George Dumezil.*
        Berkeley, Calif.: University of California Press.

——. 1970. The "kingship in heaven" theme. In *Myth and Law among
        the Indo-Europeans,* J. Puhvel, ed. Berkeley, Calif.: University
        of California Press, pp. 83-122.

Mahabharata: The Text as Constituted in its Critical Edition, 5 vols.
        1971–1975. Poona: Bhandarkar Oriental Research Institute.
        Citations translated by the author.

Mahdi, L., ed. 1987. *Betwixt and Between. Patterns of Masculine and Feminine Initiation.* LaSalle, Ill.: Open Court.

Malcom, J. 1981. *The Impossible Profession.* New York: Knopf.

Mandelbaum, A., trans. 1991. *The Odyssey.* Berkeley, Calif.: University of California Press.

Masson, J. M. 1990. *Final Analysis: The Making and Unmaking of a Psychoanalyst.* Reading, Mass.: Addison Wesley.

Miller, D. 1986. *Three Faces of God: Traces of the Trinity in Literature and Life.* Philadelphia: Fortress Press.

Moore, R. and Gillette, D. 1990. *King, Warrior, Magician, Lover: Rediscovering the Archetypes of the Mature Masculine.* San Francisco: HarperSanFrancisco.

———. 1991. *The King Within.* New York: William Morrow.

Neumann, E. 1954. *The Origins and History of Consciousness.* New York: Pantheon Books.

———. 1955. *The Great Mother: An Analysis of the Archetype.* New York: Pantheon Books.

Obeyesekhere, G. 1990. The illusory pursuit of the self—a review of *Culture and Self: Asian and Western Perspectives,* edited by Anthony J. Marsella, George DeVos, and Francis L. K. Hsu. *Philosophy East and West* 11:239–250.

Peirce, C. S. 1932. *Collected Papers,* 6 vols., C. Hartshorne and P. Weiss., eds. Cambridge, Mass.: Harvard University Press.

Perry, J. W. 1966. *Lord of the Four Quarters.* New York: Macmillan.

Pevear, R., and Volokhonsky, L., trans. 1990. *Fyodor Dostoevsky: The Brothers Karamazov.* San Francisco: North Point Press.

Pirsig, R. M. 1974. *Zen and the Art of Motorcycle Maintenance.* New York: William Morrow.

Polomé, E. 1970. The Indo-European component in Germanic religion. In *Myth and Law among the Indo-Europeans,* J. Puhvel, ed. Berkeley, Calif.: University of California Press, pp. 55–82.

Ramanujan, A. K. 1983. The Indian Oedipus. In *Oedipus: A Folklore Casebook,* L. Edmunds and A. Dundes, eds. New York: Garland Publishing.

Roland, A. 1988. *In Search of Self in India and Japan.* Princeton, N.J.: Princeton University Press.

Samuels, A. 1985. *Jung and the Post-Jungians.* London: Routledge and Kegan Paul.

Satapatha Brahmana. A. Weber, ed. Varanasi, India: Chowkambha Sanskrit Series. Citations translated by the author.

Satinover, J. 1987. Science and the fragile self: The rise of narcissism, the decline of God. In *Pathologies of the Modern Self: Postmodern Studies on Narcissism, Schizophrenia, and Depression,* D. M. Levin, ed. New York: New York University Press.

Sauvé, J. L. 1970. The divine victim: Aspects of human sacrifice in Viking Scandinavia and Vedic India. In *Myth and Law among the Indo-Europeans,* J. Puhvel, ed. Berkeley, Calif.: University of California Press, pp. 173–192.

Schwartz-Salant, N. 1987. The dead self in borderline personality disorders. In *Pathologies of the Modern Self: Postmodern Studies on Narcissism, Schizophrenia, and Depression,* D. M. Levin, ed. New York: International Universities Press.

Segal, H. 1964. *Introduction to the Work of Melanie Klein.* New York: Basic Books.

Stein, M. 1976. Narcissus. *Spring* 1976:32–53.

——. 1985. *Jung's Treatment of Christianity.* Wilmette, Ill.: Chiron Publications.

Turner, V. 1969. *The Ritual Process.* Ithaca, N.Y.: Cornell University Press.

Turville-Petre, E. O. G. 1964. *Myth and Religion of the North: The Religion of Ancient Scandinavia.* Westport, Conn.: Greenwood Press.

Twain, M. 1884. *The Adventures of Huckleberry Finn*. New York:
    Bantam Books, 1965.

van Buitenen, J. A. B. 1953. *Ramanuja on the Bhagavad Gita*.
    Gravenhage: H. L. Smitts.

———. 1981. *The Bhagavadgita in the Mahabharata*. Chicago: University
    of Chicago Press.

van Gennep, A. 1960. *The Rites of Passage*. Chicago: University of
    Chicago Press.

Whitmont, E. 1982. *The Return of the Goddess*. New York: Crossroad.

Wikander, S. 1938. *Der arische Mannerbund: Studien zur indo-
    iranischen Sprach- und Religionsgeschichte*. Lund.

Winnicott, D. W. 1971. *Playing and Reality*. London: Penguin Books.

Wylie, P. 1955. *A Generation of Vipers*. New York: Rinehart.

Zimmer, H. 1971. *The King and the Corpse: Tales of the Soul's Conquest
    of Evil*. Princeton, N.J.: Princeton University Press.

INDEX

Abraham, 4
active imagination, 30-32, 34, 136
addiction, 46-47
Agni, 104, 108-111, 119
Aitareya Aranyaka, 35
Aitareya Brahmana, 3
Allen, Woody, 63
Alper, H., 44
alter ego, 26, 38, 141
analytical psychology, 8, 23, 128
Anderson, W., 98, 140n.
anima, 13-14, 24, 30, 48, 49-51,
    53-54, 56, 58n., 60-62, 110-111,
    121, 123-124, 136, 139-142
anima mundi, 17, 51, 123, 135
animism, 135
animus, 24, 61, 142
archetypal psychology, 12, 14,
    23, 121
archetypes, 11-14, 17, 18n., 23-24,
    31-34, 42, 44, 50, 82, 84, 89-91,
    103, 111-112, 114, 119, 122-124,
    127, 133, 135-136, 140-142
    see also masculine, archetypes of
Archie Bunker, 3
Aristotle, 15, 18
Athena, 128
atman, 3, 130
Attis, 142

Bacal, H. A., 27
Baldr, 127-128
Bali, 133, 139n.
"Beauty and the Beast," 51-54, 61,
    94, 97
Beck, B. E. F., 5
Berne, Eric, 11n.
Bettelheim, B., 52-53
Bhagavad Gita, 48n., 125, 132-133
Bhisma, 131-133
Bloom, H., 11
Blumenthal, Jerome, 118n.
Bly, Robert, 24, 37, 40, 47, 87, 90,
    92-96, 98, 111, 113, 124, 126
Brahman, 90, 106-107, 117, 120,
    129-130
Brhadaranyaka Upanishad, 35, 110
Brown, Norman O., 2
Buddha, 13, 120-121

Buddhism, 4, 44-45, 102,
    120-121, 123
Bush, George, 114

Caro, Robert, 115-118, 121-122
Carstairs, M., 39
castration, 38-39, 139n., 142
Chautauqua, 14-15, 21
Chodorow, N. J., 1
Christ, 73-75
Christianity, 113, 128, 140n.
Chrysippus, 38
Colum, Padraic, 40, 92
complex(es), 11-14, 135, 140-141
    father, 12, 67
    Laius, 38-40, 42, 47
    Oedipus (oedipal), 37, 40, 42, 47,
        52, 95, 140
    son, 12
coniunctio, 29-31, 47, 50, 110-111,
    136, 138, 141
consciousness, 13, 31, 33-35, 43-44,
    46, 50, 61-62, 77, 108, 136,
    141-143
    collective, 119
    patriarchal, 134
        see also patriarchy
    Western, 15, 135
Coomaraswamy, Ananda, 5n., 88,
    108
Cosby, 3

de Man, Paul, 121-122
De Vries, L., 127, 129
death, 3-4, 19-20, 30, 37-38, 41-42,
    57, 59, 62, 66-67, 78, 83, 100, 110,
    113, 121, 124, 126-127, 129-134,
    142-143
    instinct, 32, 41-43
    wish, 41
deconstruction, 2n., 12, 84, 113-115,
    119, 121
Demeter, 142n.
depth psychology, 67
Derrida, 121-122
Desai, P., 104
Descartes, R., 17
Devavrata, 131
Devereux, G., 38-40, 48

Dimmitt, C., 105, 139n.
Dostoevsky, F., 63-64, 71, 74, 79, 83-84, 87, 89
dreams, 15-16, 18n., 20-21, 33, 37-39, 41-42, 49-51, 77-78, 80-81
Dumézil, G., 88n.
Duryodhana, 117

Eggeling, J., 109
ego, 7, 11n., 12-14, 17, 19, 23, 25, 28, 30-34, 40-44, 46, 51, 53-57, 60-62, 67, 82, 88, 91-92, 94, 96, 99, 106, 111, 136-137, 141
    dream, 20
    masculine, 49
        see also masculine
    Western, 94, 113, 119, 124
ego self, 83-84, 137
Eleusinian mysteries, 142n.
Eliade, M., 30
Ellenberger, H., 85
empathy (empathic resonance), 25-28, 30

fading, 41n., 43-44, 46, 54, 138
faith, 29-30, 34, 44-46, 59, 71, 74, 76, 80, 84
feminine (femininity), 48, 49-51, 53, 55, 60-61, 62n., 82, 94-95, 106-109, 111, 142-143
    archetype of, 49
        see also archetypes
feminism, 2, 113
    archetypal, 54n.
    literature, 62
Fitzgerald, Scott, 122
Foucault, 121
Frankfort, Henri, 90, 97, 98n., 100
Frazer, Sir James, 62
Freud, S., 8, 18, 23, 27, 37-38, 47

Gallop, J., 39, 41-42
Ganesha, 123
Gendlin, E., 33-34, 44
Gibson, J. J., 17n.
Gillette, D., 87
Gilligan, C., 1
God, 29, 50, 74-75, 81-84, 87, 91, 103, 119, 128, 137n., 138-139
    as female, 49
god(s), 49, 88n., 98, 105, 108-110, 122-123, 127-128, 132-133, 142
goddess(es), 50, 62, 107, 142n.
Goethe, 18

Goldman, Robert, 39-40, 106
Gonda, J., 101
Great Mother (Great Goddess), 62, 107, 100, 110, 138n., 139, 142
Green Man, 98, 140n.
Greenberg, 11n.
Grinnell, R., 29
guru, 4-5, 14, 22, 40, 48n., 60, 74, 85, 106n., 121

Hades, 142
Hanly, P., 8
Harivamsa, 118
Hasan, Abu Zayd, 101
Havamal, 129
Heesterman, J. C., 118
Heidegger, 41n., 119
Hemingway, Ernest, 122
heterosexuality, 48, 68
Hicks, C., 98, 140n.
Hillman, James, 7, 11-14, 16-17, 18n., 21-24, 27, 31-34, 47, 49-50, 58, 61, 87, 92, 94, 98-100, 121-124, 135, 139, 142
Hinduism, 44-45, 49-50, 62, 103, 120, 123, 138
Hocart, A. M., 90
Hodr, 127-128
Homans, 8n.
Homer Simpson, 3
homosexuality, 38-40, 46, 48
Horus, 97-100
Houston, Sam, 115
hubris, 127-128
Huck Finn, see The Adventures of Huckleberry Finn
hysteria, 58, 60

I Ching, 3, 63
immortality, 3, 61, 104, 127, 129, 131
incest, 46-48
Inden, Ronald, 91n., 100-105, 107, 117, 120n.
India, 4, 17n., 22, 29-31, 35, 39, 41n., 43, 45, 48n., 62, 67, 82, 88n., 90, 91n., 100, 102, 105-107, 110, 117-118, 120, 122, 126, 129, 131, 133, 137-138, 141
individuation, 1, 8n., 13-14, 23, 34, 142
Indra, 108, 117
inflation, 13, 17, 24, 81, 96, 133

initiation, 40, 53, 64, 76, 80, 87, 89, 92, 94-95, 99, 122-124, 126-130, 132-134
introspection, 27-28
Irigaray, L., 62, 113
"Iron John," 92-95, 99, 106
Isis, 97, 100

Job, Book of, 128
Johnson, Lyndon, 114-119, 121-122
Johnson, Sam Ealy, 115-116
Johnson, Sam Houston, 116
Joseph, S., 42n.
Jung, C. G., 1, 7-8, 11-14, 22-24, 25, 27-35, 37, 40, 44, 49, 90-92, 96, 119, 128, 135, 137n., 141-142
Jung, Paul, 22

Kali, 62
Kamsa, 117
Katha Upanishad, 129-130
Kazin, Alfred, 66n.
Kerenyi, K., 142
Kierkegaard, S., 1, 87
king, *see* masculine, archetypes of
King Lear, 4n., 55-61, 69, 87, 97, 106-107
King Midas, 96, 138
kingship (kinghood), 90-91, 93-94, 97-98, 100-101, 103-105, 114, 128n., 131-133, 138
    demonic, 106-107, 118
    Indian, 100-107, 112, 115, 119
Klein, M., 29
Knipe, D., 110-111
Kohut, Heinz, 7-8, 16, 24, 25-30, 34n., 44, 46, 89-90, 96, 105, 135-137, 140-141, 143
Kore, 142
Krishna, 132-133
Kronos, 128n.

Lacan, J., 38, 41-43, 121
Laius, 39, 46, 92, 127, 131
Larson, G. J., 43
Lehman, David, 2n., 121-122
Lévi-Strauss, C., 47-48, 56
Lewis, C. S. , 114
Lipner, J., 103
Littleton, C. Scott, 88n., 128n.
love, 3, 11, 13-14, 21, 24, 38, 40, 51-56, 58, 73, 75, 77, 83-85, 87, 91, 96, 105, 116, 122

Mahabharata, 39, 101, 131
Mahdi, L., 37
Mahisha, 138-139n.
Malcolm, J., 2n.
Marcuse, Herbert, 2
masculine (masculinity), 37, 40, 49, 51, 89, 94, 98-99, 106, 111-112, 134, 142-143
    archetype of, 50, 88n.
        king, 87-112, 113-115, 117-122
        lover, 88-89
        magician, 88-90, 115, 122
        warrior, 88-89, 118
masochism, 88
Masson, J. M., 2n., 8
matriarchy, 62, 98-99
Meade, Michael, 87
Meister Eckhart, 137n.
men's movement, 87
Merlin, 96
mistletoe, 127
Mitchell, 11n.
monism, 135
Moore, Robert, 87-92, 94, 101, 103, 106, 111-112, 114, 122, 126, 141, 143
mother, 8n., 11, 29, 39, 47-48, 56, 58, 89, 98-99, 108, 122, 136, 140, 142
    see also Great Mother
mother–infant domain, 1
murder, 5, 22, 38, 53, 59, 61, 63, 67-68, 76, 80-81, 127
    guru, 4
    soul, 5
myth, 3, 24, 30, 39, 47, 62, 97-99, 105-106, 127, 143
mythology, Indian, 138n.
    see also India, Indian gods and goddesses by name

Naciketas, 129-131
narcissism, 8, 68, 96, 127
narcissistic personality disorder, 28, 112
Neumann, Erich, 8n., 62n., 90, 98-99, 142
Nicholas, R., 102
nigredo, 30-32, 41, 43, 47

Obeyesekhere, G., 121
object relations theory, 11n., 29
Odin, 127-129, 131